GAINING PUBLIC TRUST
A Profile of Civic Engagement

GAINING PUBLIC TRUST:

A Profile of Civic Engagement

By
Former Seattle Mayor
NORMAN B. RICE

ENDICOTT
and HUGH
BOOKS

Front cover: Seattle Skyline: Austin Wehrwein, Norm Rice photo: Constance Rice
Editors: Jeanie Okimoto and Amy Kirkman
Book and Cover design: Masha Shubin
Seattle Municipal Archives photos: Seattle Municipal Archives photos: 176746, 174671, 77387, 174675, 77973, 77971, 174669, 173769, 174663, 77382, 174178, 173317, 174062, 174063, 173874, 77381, 77392, 173982, 174014, 173329, 174033, 173043, 7796, 77975, 77974, 171933
Campaign photos: Joel Levin
Coalition photo: Kathleen King

Names: Rice, Norman B., author.
Title: Gaining public trust : a profile of civic engagement / by former Seattle Mayor, Norman B. Rice.
Description: Burton, Washington : Endicott and Hugh Books, [2020] | Includes bibliographical references.
Identifiers: ISBN 9780999364642 (trade paperback)
Subjects: LCSH: Rice, Norman B.--Career in public administration. | African American mayors--Washington (State)--Seattle--Biography. | Seattle (Wash.)--Politics and government--20th century. | Political participation--Washington (State)--Seattle. | LCGFT: Autobiographies.
Classification: LCC F899.S453 R53 2020 | DDC 979.777204092--dc23

Proceeds from
Gaining Public Trust: A Profile in Civic Engagement
are donated to the Northwest African American Museum

ISBN: 978-0-9993646-4-2 Trade paperback

Printed in the United States of America

1 3 5 7 9 10 8 6 4 2

To Mama Powell, Constance, and Mian...my true trinity.

CONTENTS

ACKNOWLEDGMENTS

It is often said success has many mothers and fathers, but failure is an orphan. At the end of the day, these are the people I love and care about who were always there for me: Mama Powell, Constance Rice, Mian Rice, Bob Watt, and Joe and Jeanie Okimoto.

FOREWORD

When Norm Rice was elected mayor of Seattle, it was the most divisive, polarized time in the city's history. African Americans were only 10 percent of the city's population and Norm's election was ground-breaking. It was 1989 and the city was torn apart over the issue of busing to achieve school desegregation. On the same ballot with Norm was an anti-busing initiative. The anti-busing measure passed, Norm Rice was elected, and became the mayor of a city tearing itself apart.

What followed was an exemplary demonstration of leadership as Norm Rice brought a divided city together and went on to accomplish historic changes and improvements. Praising Rice as one of the best mayors Seattle has ever had, a *Seattle Times* editorial upon his retirement as CEO of the Seattle Foundation observed, "rare is the public leader who manages to be highly effective and well-regarded. Rice has been both." His skilled leadership was aided in part by a keen, analytical mind where he could quickly assess the core or essence of any situation. But most importantly, Norm Rice was, and is—a person of great warmth, humor, and generosity of spirit. With an extraordinary memory for names and faces (an enviable gift for any politician) he made everyone he met feel special. He was expressive and appreciative in affirming other people and quick to recognize their value. His great strength was in attracting a group of exceptionally talented people who shared his values and worked tirelessly with him to carry out their shared vision for Seattle.

No one had a closer front row seat than Deputy Mayor Bob Watt. "I was privileged to be part of this journey, to watch from the inside as the soul of this man found ways to listen to everyone, help them see the common threads in their unique hopes and dreams and then weave those common threads into lasting solutions that changed our city, Seattle, for the better.

As Norman recounts in this book so movingly, he learned critical lessons in leadership from his Denver family of origin and their sometimes challenging circumstances. Rather than be diminished by failure, he took important lessons from those failures and moved beyond them, wiser and undaunted. When the love of his life and his soul mate Constance came into his world, he found a way to be sure she stayed in his life forever, and together they grew in love and leadership.

And when the time came for him to lead a city beyond divisiveness into action based on hope, he was ready. Ready to extend all that he had learned into a listening process that captured all the positive energy of so many of Seattle's citizens, while also engaging and respecting the negative and fearful emotions felt by many. Ready to take that careful listening and turn it into concrete actions that would benefit all Seattle's children and families for decades to come.

The Rice administration is perhaps best known for the Education Summit process and the resultant Families and Education Levy. But that same process was used over and over and this book touches on some of those processes too. Whether it was creating a comprehensive plan or figuring out what it would take to turn a dying downtown into a thriving downtown, the same principles were at work. Listen, really listen. See the common threads, not just your own hopes and fears. Develop a plan of action *with* the people affected. Act on the plan, so that trust and credibility are continuously created because when you are leading a city there will always be another reason to change the way things are.

One final principle that Norman exemplifies so well: Keep your own soul and the souls of those around you well fed and growing. Why? The trials and temptations of life, especially when you are leading, are wearying. Succumbing helps no one. I never once saw Norman Rice succumb."

In describing Norm Rice's leadership, Sandra Archibald, former Dean of the Evans School of Public Policy and Governance at the University of Washington observed, "He has always led with a focus on collaboration, courage, respect, and integrity. It's no wonder that he engendered such broad public support during his many years of public service and beyond."

The lessons Norm Rice learned about civic engagement have never been needed more. Gaining public trust is critical if our cities and our country can overcome crises, meet challenges, and move ahead to improve the quality of life where each and every citizen can flourish. With candor and wisdom, Norm Rice chronicles his journey to leadership and public service, and reflects on the lessons he learned about civic engagement through his remarkable success in bringing a divided city together. We are privileged to publish his story.

Endicott and Hugh Books

INTRODUCTION

In the face of impossible odds, people who love this country can change it.

- Barack Obama

I was inspired to write about civic engagement because I believe that even under the most divisive and trying circumstances, people can be engaged to find the common denominator that brings them together. People are more engaged by politics now than at any time since the Vietnam War. They're taking to the streets and staging protests all over the country. Anger is a great motivator for getting involved, but being involved in protests and politics is very different from being involved in governing. The job of leadership is to help people get from "woke" to work.

People have always gathered to talk about issues facing their communities. We do it at dinner parties, in the town square, and on the front stoop. These days we do it on a computer or a phone. But what's changed from the days of the town square or front stoop gatherings from our past is today we can block out anyone who doesn't share our worldview. It's not like the days when people read newspapers, watched the news on TV, or listened to radio broadcasts and then hammered out solutions around the water cooler at work. Before cable news and the proliferation of talk radio, people would watch and read the news hoping whatever was happening in the world would reinforce their own political beliefs. Now, it seems we all go straight to those information platforms that reinforce our own preconceptions.

We're not often listening to diverse opinions. At most we're reading them in 140 or 280 characters and sending off not very nuanced retorts. While we might feel more engaged with the advent of social media, this kind of interaction really has nothing to do with real civic engagement. The question we face is whether communities can harness the anger and inspire people to connect on local issues in constructive, deliberative, and positive interaction. Of course, I say the answer is yes. I base this on my idealism and positive perspectives about human nature and our responses to find the best in others. I also say now is a good time to renew our dedication to involving people in decisions that affect their lives. There is no better example of extreme engagement than the recent March For Our Lives, orchestrated by students affected by gun violence and the nation-wide protests against racial injustice in the wake of the killing of George Floyd.

People really do care deeply about issues in their communities. If elected officials learn how to inspire them, they can be brought into the governing process in a meaningful way. People will actually take the next step in participatory government and show up. But it is imperative to foster an environment where citizens feel a sense of ownership in public policy and have a safe space to express their views freely. An engaged citizenry is a fundamental component in healthy communities, and that aspect of governing needs to be promoted and nurtured.

We need both civic and *civil* engagement. The skeptics among us might look around and say there is no chance for civic engagement that is civil these days because our politics have become so divisive. But I don't believe that. I believe democracy survives only when we have meaningful engagement of the populace. It takes more than just voting or reading polling data. It is imperative to examine what it means to participate civilly in the political process and go back to the days when we actually solved problems by listening to each other and arriving at solutions together. It isn't even so much a matter of bringing bi-partisanship into the mix; it has more to do with people recognizing we all approach problems differently. Reaching agreement on the problem is just one step. We have to then find a way forward, despite our differences, to get to the solutions that work best.

During my years in public service, both as a city council member and as mayor, I was in a position of leadership in dealing with many local issues, but none were as tough as the controversy surrounding busing to achieve school desegregation. It was at its most divisive when I was elected mayor. Our approach to bringing a divided community together began with convening meetings in every neighborhood in the city to listen to all citizens. We called it the Education Summit and we hoped to identify shared values which then could lead to solutions that most people could support. It was a huge undertaking and it involved countless people—volunteers from all over the city, as well as everyone on our staff—and they gave it their all to make it happen. They are too numerous to thank, but it is because of them that the Education Summit became a reality.

We learned to engage citizens in a manner that respects diversity of opinion and we learned to bring them together in a way that was goal oriented—not grievance oriented. The process and how we developed solutions became a model for us in going forward to deal with many other issues facing the city.

In writing about how we used civic engagement to solve problems during my tenure as mayor, I don't claim to have all the answers. But what I hope to provide is a blueprint for coming together to solve a common problem using engagement as the most effective tool in building strong communities. It can't be overstated: In a democracy, it is imperative the real work starts after the election and it involves pulling citizens together over common interests. It is more important now than ever that we understand principles for civic engagement, and it is to that end that I am sharing my journey in public service and what I have learned.

Norman B. Rice

PART I

A JOURNEY TO LEADERSHIP

Norm Rice taking oath of office as Mayor with Constance and Mian Rice.

A TURNING POINT

In his poem "Harlem" Langston Hughes asks what happens when we lose sight of our dreams. "What happens to a dream deferred?" he asks. "Does it dry up, like a raisin in the sun? Or fester like a sore--and then run? Does it stink like rotten meat or crust and sugar-over like a syrupy sweet? Maybe it just sags like a heavy load. *Or does it explode?*" "Harlem" was the inspiration for the name and themes in Lorraine Hansberry's critically acclaimed and Tony Award-winning play *A Raisin in the Sun*. Both the poem and the play had such a profound impact on my personal and public journey, it informed the major underpinnings of my political and professional life.

I was a young man on April 4, 1968, working as an engineer's assistant at IBM in Boulder, Colorado, and performing nights and weekends in community and professional theater. I remember my supervisor came to me with the news that Rev. Martin Luther King, Jr. had been assassinated. I didn't know what to do. He told me I could go home if I wished, but I told him it was okay. I thought I would stay at work. At that time in my life, acting was a passion that filled my evenings and weekends, and as fate would have it, I was appearing in a production of *A Raisin in the Sun* the night of Dr. King's assassination. Once the weight of the news really sunk in, I told my supervisor that I would, indeed, like to go home. But I didn't want to go home. I got in my car and started driving. I ended up at the theater where the cast was already gathering.

I couldn't have told you then what a monumental influence the two events would have on my life going forward, nor could I tell you then where it would lead. But looking back, hearing the news of Dr. King's death and performing that very night in a play about the deferred dreams of Black people, set off something profound in me that ended up changing my life forever.

Despite having flunked out of the University of Colorado, I was making my way in the world and doing just fine, thank you, when Dr. King died. My resume was solid, I had good references, and the job at IBM provided me an empowering sense of employment security. I'm confident had I chosen to remain on that path, I likely would have advanced in the company enough to carve out a pretty decent future. I'm an optimistic fellow and so I was happy enough. The job was solid and acting gave me a creative outlet, fulfilling what was, I guess, a subconscious need to be in the spotlight. So yes, life was sailing along smoothly in the spring of 1968. But something just hadn't quite fallen into place for me. I certainly wasn't driven, either at work or on the stage. The work I was doing at IBM was sometimes interesting, but nothing, not even the acting, was inspiring me on to bigger and better things.

For people of color all over America, the days and weeks following Dr. King's assassination was a time of great reflection, anger, grief, and, for some, profound soul-searching. It was no different for me. The circumstances of performing in that play, constantly mulling the theme of dreams unrealized, being totally immersed in the unfulfilled lives of those characters, and King's death all came together like a tsunami after an earthquake. It caused me to wonder about my own dreams. Was I fulfilling them, or at least on a path to that end? I pondered those questions that spring and summer and eventually came to the truth: My dreams were taking a back seat to the day-to-day realities of paying the rent and putting food on the table. If I wasn't careful, soon my dreams would no longer be a factor in my life or they would morph into something else, something lesser.

In my youth, I frequently imagined myself as a leader. I had always been a peacemaker in my family, and I had successfully politicked and won a couple of school elections. Somehow I always knew I had the right instincts for leadership. Even as a child, I had a need to convince people to like me and believe what I was telling them. I ran for and served in student government all through high school. I went to Boys State and then on to Boys Nation in Washington, DC. It felt good to make people listen to me. I was a confident young man when it came to my leadership skills and so I think, in a way, I always was destined for public service. I could have been a leader at IBM. But if I stayed and worked my way up the management ladder, would that be enough?

A period of intense self-reflection began for me while crying backstage with the rest of the cast that darkest of dark spring nights in 1968. And in the course of that reflection, I soon realized that no matter how secure I felt at my job in Boulder, no matter how much fun I was having onstage, I wasn't living my dream. I was getting by. I was working a job, and acting part time. But I wanted and needed more. I needed to find my passion.

As spring turned to summer that year, the desire to make meaningful changes in my life grew stronger and stronger. A visit to my mother's cousin in Tacoma earlier allowed me to take stock of my life. Surrounded by some of the most beautiful geography in the country, I gained a fresh perspective. Cousin Dorothy said if I was looking to make a change, I would be welcome to live with her until I got on my feet. So late in the so-called summer of love, I gave my notice at IBM, packed up my car, said my good-byes, and headed to the Pacific Northwest.

NEW LIFE:
New Chapters

The early years in Seattle gave me valuable experience for my future in public service. While I was getting my bachelor's degree in communications, followed by my master's at the Evans School of Public Policy and Governance at University of Washington, I had jobs in both the private and public sectors. Among them, Seattle Freeholder, Executive Aide with Puget Sound Council of Governments, Assistant Director of the Urban League of Metropolitan Seattle, a reporter with KOMO TV and KIXI radio, and Manager of Charitable Corporate Contributions and Community Relations at Rainier National Bank. And as president of a neighborhood organization, the Mt. Baker Community Club, I gained experience in community engagement at the grass roots level.

Ten years after leaving Denver, I had a master's degree in public administration, had met and married my soul mate and love of my life, Dr. Constance Williams Acholonu, and had won the election to my first term on the Seattle City Council, beating a huge field of candidates. All of this tells you the significance of my decision to leave the place I had always known to forge a new future. Dreams no longer deferred.

EARLY DAYS OF PUBLIC SERVICE:
The Seattle City Council

On November 7, 1978 the City of Seattle held a special election to fill the unexpired term of council member Phyllis Lamphere who resigned in August of that year to take a position with the US Economic Development Agency. Community activist, Delores Sibonga was appointed to fill Phyllis's unexpired term, agreeing not to run for the seat she was appointed to fill. Wayne Larkin, who had resigned his seat to run for mayor the previous year, ran for the seat, along with thirteen others.

I jumped into the political water in a special election against fourteen candidates for that city council seat. In addition to my academic study of public administration, my experience as reporter, work at the Urban League where I conducted a study of the future of minority cable TV ownership, and my work on the City Charter Committee all brought me to the race with a solid background in public policy. Other positions also provided me a ready-made base of support. I was president of the Mt. Baker Community Council and, as the manager of social engagement for Rainier Bank, I came in daily contact with top executives in the city, so I had some business cred as well. I had strong connections in the neighborhoods and in the city at large. A diverse base of support, combined with decent name recognition, led to me winning that race.

I remained on the Seattle City Council for eleven years.

My city council tenure was a time of great personal and political growth. It was an exciting time to enter the council, as minorities were just beginning to play a role in city government and I very much wanted to be a part of that. Sam Smith was the first African American elected to the council in 1967 and I was the second, elected over ten years later. I was eager to absorb as much as I could about policy and public service. I also wanted to learn about leadership because making change and being a positive force for my community was my goal. It was never my goal as a council member to make a big splash in politics.

I worked hard those first years on the council but kept a fairly low profile. I was serious about learning and governing as opposed to politicking. As my experience on the council grew, I am happy to say I developed a reputation as someone who would consider all angles of an issue and go about the work of governing in a thoughtful and deliberative manner. That comes from being a pragmatic optimist or a pragmatic liberal, however you want to look at it. I will not fight to the death on an issue. Understanding and drilling down on the matter at hand is more important than fighting to the death. It's better to be roughly right than precisely wrong. If you constantly have a knee-jerk reaction to issues, then your concern looks disingenuous. If you bring people together on an issue, despite different solutions offered, then you can tell the story to everyone more effectively.

In those years, the city council members were elected at large and the beauty of the at-large council system was that it pulled together a diversity of people and views and issues from all over the city. I thought it was a mistake for the city to go to single member districts because it leads to dealing with fractious neighborhood squabbles rather than citywide issues.

I was now a Seattle City Council member and I was very serious about the work. I learned a great deal about the council, about building consensus, and about compromise. I'm convinced that because I didn't have an agenda going into office, I was approachable on most issues. I never have been an ideologue and that gave me a certain flexibility I believe served me well.

The first committee appointments on the council were pretty straightforward administrative assignments. Since I ran my campaign as a policy wonk, I didn't have a bunch of flashy or empty campaign promises I had to manage. I ran as a neighborhood activist and a human rights proponent, but I didn't have a particular matter to promote. Instead, I delved into subjects that came before my committees. As time went on, the committees became more significant, the issues more broad. I worked on utilities, land use questions, economic development, financial management, and housing. No matter what committee assignment I had or what issues we dealt with, every matter that came before me was one more learning experience in knowing the value of input from all stakeholders, not just civic leaders and experts.

I served for four years as chair of the Finance and Budget Committee, and my proudest accomplishment on that committee was the enactment of the Women and Minority Business Enterprise Ordinance which mandated the city give contract preference to women and minority-owned businesses. It was a huge move forward in our effort to help those businesses compete on an equal footing with other, more established companies.

Seattle City Council group portrait January 15, 1985

FRIENDS AND CONFIDANTS

I met a lot of people in the time leading up to my city council run, but it was during my first term on the council that I met Bob Watt. Bob's background was in social work and when we met he was President and CEO of Family Services of Seattle/ King County. We quickly became friends and our friendship has lasted all these years. Our sons were both soccer players, so we had that in common. We also shared political views, a deep commitment to family and community, and a love of public service.

Mayor Charley Royer called on Bob to head up the KidsPlace Action Agenda process, a major, city-sponsored effort to make Seattle known more broadly as a kid-friendly city. Obviously, schools were a part of that effort because the entire endeavor was geared to attracting business to Seattle, and all businesses look at the education climate in a city before making crucial relocation plans.

During my time on the council, my relationship with Mayor Royer could accurately be described as somewhat rocky. It's not that we clashed all the time, but the disagreements we had were not insignificant. Nonetheless, my name came up to serve on the KidsPlace Initiative basically no one expected me to serve because of the frosty relationship I had with Royer. But Bob wanted me to work with him, so he asked, and I was happy to join what was a worthy endeavor that involved issues I cared deeply about. I served as chair of the education section of the initiative, which greatly increased my knowledge of the workings of the Seattle School District. It was instrumental in giving me the expertise, support system, and knowledge I would need later when education in Seattle would take center stage.

Bob and I bonded even more, as both friends and colleagues, during our service together the KidsPlace Iniative. Every turn in my political career from then on involved Bob, as it did Constance, and friends Bob Gogerty, Walt Crowley, and Charles Rolland. These five people, and my son Mian as he grew up, became my inner circle. They were the people I trusted most in the world, beginning with Constance. I could always count on Constance to be the one to tap me on the shoulder and call me out if I needed it and I rely on her strength and judgment still.

PROGRESS ON THE COUNCIL
AND DEFEAT AT THE POLLS

The year 1980 was not a good year for Democrats anywhere in the country, and that was true for Washington State. Ronald Reagan had just been elected president and Washington had elected a Republican governor and a Republican United States Senator. In the GOP sweep that year, fishing company heir Slade Gorton defeated long time popular progressive incumbent Senator Warren G. Magnuson for his senate seat.

Between 1980 and 1985, I continued to work on a variety of tough issues mainly dealing with social justice, economic development, strong neighborhoods, and economic justice. I am proud of that work, but I was still at odds with the mayor on a range of topics, so with Constance and Bob Watt by my side, I decided in 1985 to challenge Charley Royer in that year's mayoral race.

Running as a policy wonk for city council had served me well, so that's what I decided to do in the mayoral race. It was a mistake. I remember going to the first debate, all buttoned up in my suit and tie and Charley came in and casually took off his jacket and wasn't wearing a tie. He looked like Mr. Regular Guy and I looked like a banker. Terry Wittman and Tom Hujar co-managed that campaign, and Hujar wanted me to come off more strident and aggressive in the debates—but that just wasn't me. I never could pull that off well. I took a huge binder filled with policy positions and information to the debate and thought I was all ready to go. I was ready for a lecture series in some classroom, perhaps, but having a binder full of research or policy statements was not a good plan in the mayor's race.

Looking back, I remember that night as a local version of the Kennedy-Nixon debate, and although I don't think there was sweat coming down my face, I was stiff and uncomfortable and not at all spontaneous. I ended up losing that election. An article in the *New York Times* explored the political climate in Seattle at the time and the conclusion was that it was not exactly what one would call an exciting campaign. "There are few other issues in the campaign to lead city government in Seattle, where times are generally good, unemployment is relatively low, taxes are not too oppressive and the downtown is undergoing a construction boom. Except for some debate on the future of the city's baseball franchise and a September schools strike, there have been few of the sharp exchanges that make for lively campaigns.

The nonpartisan election will be November 5. The candidates, both Democrats, are survivors of an eight-candidate primary that Mr. Royer led with 56 percent of the vote. Mr. Rice ran second with 34 percent. The 77,000 votes cast represented only 23.3 percent of the registered voters."[1]

The loss in that campaign was tough. If you've never run for public office, I'm not sure you can genuinely know what it feels like to lose. For one thing, losing a political campaign is a very public failure. It's kind of like being slapped in the face in front of thousands of people. You feel rejected, embarrassed, and there's no glossing over the pain. This loss almost pushed me out of politics altogether.

After recovering from the loss, if I were to name the single most important lesson I learned from that campaign, it would be that it's not what you *know*, but what you *think* that matters in public service. Yes, you have to know the issues, but you have to have an instinct for wanting to do the right thing and you have to have actual original thoughts about issues, not just what briefing papers tell you.

If I could put my finger on a problem I see with many elected officials these days, it is that they don't do their homework. You have to know what you're talking about, take time for thoughtful reflection, do your research, and try to listen to all interested parties. All the binders in the world cannot help you if you don't know the issues. You cannot work to make people's lives and communities better if you don't understand the obstacles and problems confronting those communities.

The most powerful moment in the George W. Bush presidency was what became known as his "bullhorn moment." He stood in New York City, amidst the rubble of the Twin Towers with a mega phone and someone in the crowd yelled, "We can't hear you." Bush responded by saying these now famous words "I can hear you. The rest of the world hears you! And the people—and the people who knocked these buildings down will hear all of us soon." In that instant, he told people he understood. It was the most significant utterance of his presidency.

As the "bullhorn moment" exemplifies, people really just want to be heard. Not just their complaints and desires, but also their ideas and suggestions. After my defeat, I started to take the art of listening even more seriously than I had in the past. I listened to people, I listened to experts, I read position papers, and I did research. As I learned and grew as a council member, the most important quality I developed was the ability to reach out to citizens and understand their thoughts, concerns, and dreams. I heard them and I acted on what they were telling me. That's what you can do if you understand what they're telling you, know what the issues are, and have a reasonable under-standing of possible solutions. Constituents will get engaged when they know their words matter— when they know you've been hearing what they're saying, and when they know you're working on a solution. Then, when people realize involvement makes change happen, they get invested and turn to their public servants for leadership. As someone once told me, "People don't elect managers. They elect leaders."

After my unsuccessful bid in the mayoral race, I returned to the city council and continued to work in the areas of education, diversity, growth and economic development, crime prevention, and human rights. I was disappointed by the loss, but still had a range of issues I was passionate about and there was plenty of work to do as a council member.

The decade of 1979 to 1989 saw great change in our city. For one thing, Seattle was growing fast, although not nearly to the extent it is now, and we desperately needed to manage that growth as much as possible. I felt with planning, economic development, and citizen input we could make growth a posi-tive thing. The way I see it, growth can bring positive energy and development to minority and low-income neighborhoods *if* it's not seen as a way to push people out of their communities for the economic benefit of a few rich developers. It was important to me then, just as it is now, that growth in Seattle benefit everyone and not displace people from their neighborhoods. Those same issues are greatly exaggerated now that Seattle has become one of the fasting growing cities in the nation.

In 1988, Congressman Mike Lowry decided to run for US Senate and that opened up the District 7 Congressional seat. It had been three years since my loss in the mayoral race and I guess time heals all wounds because, inspired in part by the presidential candidacy of Jesse Jackson and the Rainbow Coa-lition, I decided to enter the Democratic primary for Congress.

I called on Charles Rolland who led the Rainbow Coalition and Jesse Jackson's successful presidential primary campaign in Washington State. An article in the *Seattle Times* the day following the primary heralded Jackson's success.

"The real Democratic celebration was a few blocks up in the Central Area, where dozens of Jesse Jackson's faithful were tallying their numbers, dancing to a boom-box and issuing group raspberries to network reports of Albert Gore's 'surprise' wins in some southern states. According to their numbers, Jackson had swept Seattle's liberal 37th and 43rd districts, as expected. However, he also was winning a plurality of delegates in the less liberal 11th, 32nd, and 46th, and in Whatcom County and Thurston County. A statewide sampling put Dukakis and Jackson in a virtual tossup—Dukakis with an estimated 40 percent of the delegates, Jackson with 38 percent, the rest divided among other candidates and uncommitted delegates.

'This is Jesse's day,' announced Ellie Menzies, a Jackson organizer. It was simple grass-roots work—hundreds of volunteers and caucus-training sessions—that enabled them to go head-to-head with a well-financed Dukakis campaign,' she said."[2]

Charles Rolland and the Rainbow Coalition had done an amazing job with the Jackson campaign, pulling together a huge coalition of Democratic voters. It was a real coup he pulled off in that primary, and it was a hopeful time for Democrats in Seattle. I was optimistic about my chances in the Democratic primary for Congress. The *Seattle Times* covered my announcement on March 30.

"'The goals of the Reagan administration don't meet America's needs and must be changed,' Seattle City Councilman Norm Rice said today, in formally announcing his candidacy for a seat in Congress. 'The very fabric of our community's quality of life, the things that make this region a special place to live, are being threatened by federal neglect and misguided federal priorities,' said Rice, in entering the race to succeed Rep. Mike Lowry in the 7th Congressional District."[3]

The primary for the nomination, one of the last in the country, was held on Tuesday, September 20. It was a three-way race: myself, Jim McDermott, and King County Assessor, Ruth Ridder. We were all competing to replace Lowry who won his primary to face the GOP candidate for US Senate in November. That night, McDermott took the lead early on and the results never changed. The next day, the *Seattle Times* captured the mood of our campaign. "Tears were flowing in the Rice campaign headquarters, where disappointed supporters embraced and talked about future plans for their candidate. 'I'm blessed in one way. I still have a job,' said Rice. The crowd then chanted, 'Mayor Rice, Mayor Rice.'"

I told them then I had no other political plans except to continue working on city matters I cared deeply about and I was determined to press forward. I wanted to work on the children's and family initiative; we desperately needed to fix police-community relations, and there were increasing issues surrounding the public school system. After a decade of busing to achieve racial integration, the system was coming under fire from the largely white population in Seattle and an undercurrent of dissatisfaction and mistrust was simmering just below the surface.

After yet another political defeat, I had no desire to ever run for office again. I gathered my closest supporters together in May and told them I would not be running for mayor, despite the enthusiasm for such a bid among them. Little did I know that in just two months, one single issue would cause such divisiveness in our community that I would reconsider my decision.

THE MOST DIVISIVE ISSUE

In a strange twist of fate, the issue of school busing for racial integration swirled around the mayoral race in 1989 and, as you might expect, it was getting ugly. One of the candidates was instrumental in drafting a ballot initiative to do away with busing all together as a means of integrating Seattle Public Schools. That ballot initiative, to ban busing, was the cornerstone of his campaign. The other candidates, claiming it was a school district issue and not a city issue, all but ignored it. But for the people of Seattle, the concern for lack of academic improvement and poor schools, as well as busing, led to a rallying cry for many citizens and the rhetoric was getting heated.

Having lost an election for mayor and a race for Congress, I was convinced my marketability was wanting and deficient. However, I became more and more concerned about the divisiveness the initiative was causing. It was like a red flag to me.

I kept waiting for someone in the race to bring reason and sanity to the playing field and hoping that the logic and common sense would lead citizens to reject the initiative. Either those voices were muted or they silently supported the busing ban because the polls were showing the initiative was going to pass. Most of the candidates running for mayor knew that and, since they did not consider it the purview of the city, they punted on the issue. It seemed as though people wanted to vote for the busing ban but didn't know how to engage civilly on the issue of busing to achieve racial integration.

The issue was crying for leadership. I could not leave it alone, nor did I have the attitude that it was merely a school district problem. A group of African American community leaders, me included, came out against the measure three days before the filing deadline. The *Seattle Times* reported, "A new group, whose members are some of Seattle's most prominent Black leaders and organizations, says Initiative 34 threatens race relations in the city. The Seattle School District's 'controlled choice' desegregation plan should be allowed a chance to work before it is preempted by the initiative, said leaders of Citizens in Opposition to Initiative 34. The group announced its formation this week.

'I don't think there's any question that the initiative would re-segregate the schools,' said Urban League President R.Y. Woodhouse, who is acting as spokeswoman for the new group. The initiative is going to hurt race relations in this city.'

'It's already doing that,' said TJ Vassar, President of the Seattle School Board."[4]

What does someone who's always dreamed of being a courageous leader do when he or she believes a policy initiative is divisive, fails to bring thought and reason to the fore, and despite being just plain wrong appears destined to pass? You summon the political will and enter the fray. Thank God for righteous indignation because here I was, the council member who was never going to seek higher office, and who was going to be content serving on the council, entering a mayoral race in one of the most turbulent times in the history of a city that prides itself on progressive politics and diversity. What does one do when rhetoric and emotions run high, anger exposes hatred and bigotry, and proposals and solutions offered foster yet more and deeper divisions?

About twenty minutes before the filing deadline, I announced my candidacy and dove into the primary race for mayor because no other candidate was addressing the angry split occurring in our city. It was becoming one of the most contentious issues facing the city of Seattle since I moved there in the late 1960s. I know jumping in to the race like I did angered some of my colleagues. I think everyone thought that since I had run twice and lost I would never run again. That's what I thought as well. But everyone else was punting on the busing issue and I was increasingly angry and disappointed over the tenor of the debate. As I said when I announced my candidacy, "Above all, I listened for the words that would soothe the divisions among us, that would lift our civic spirits, and would bind our urban family closer. You and I have not heard those words. The needs of our community have not been given the full, clear voice they deserve. Rather than words of vision, we have all heard new, shrill voices of division—setting community against community, neighborhood against neighborhood, institution against institution, and most alarming of all, race against race."[5]

Seattle Public Schools were facing a crisis of confidence for a variety of reasons but the dissatisfaction reached a boiling point when voters were asked to repeal the busing plan that had, just ten years earlier, been a source of community pride. Despite facing a bevy of lawsuits, Seattle was never court-ordered to bus our students to achieve racial integration and we were proud of having taken the initiative to come up with a busing plan ourselves.

It felt like Initiative 34 was burning a hole in my city. The measure provided that six percent of all city revenues would go to the school system to end busing as a means to achieve racial balance. The money would offset the loss of federal dollars for failing to have a plan to integrate our public schools. The rhetoric surrounding the busing ban was growing more and more incendiary by the time I jumped into the race.

The mayoral contest attracted a huge field of candidates that year, including the Republican author of the anti-busing initiative—and still not one of them was discussing it. The busing issue had been smoldering on the outskirts of city politics for a while. Yes, it was a school district issue and the schools were not under the auspices of city government, but it was dividing the community and I felt strongly it should be addressed in the mayor's race, so I stepped in. Most of the candidates, as I said, simply refused to address the issue and dismissed it as not a municipal issue.

When I first entered the race, the stanza of bringing people together resonated, but the question lingered. "To do what?" No matter how evident it is that the bias of race and class lingers, finding unifying strategies were still elusive. The primary debates focused on whether school policy in general was the business of the city, so the busing issue became the elephant in the room. Although my persistence on the matter propelled me to advance to the general election, it was apparent a large number of Seattle voters wanted busing to end.

For the campaign, we put together a coalition of Democrats who had supported Jesse Jackson in the 1988 election (known as the Rainbow Coalition), white liberals, and people in the business community who didn't want the anti-busing rhetoric to define Seattle. But make no mistake: No one truly "loved" busing, even liberals and people of color. However, the split made for divisive and tone-deaf forums on the issue. What most people have forgotten was the effectiveness of the Jesse Jackson campaign for president. The caucus machine it put together to capture the primary votes in King County and Washington State was one of the most sophisticated and robust efforts I had ever seen. My campaign spoke to the core values of those individuals and they came on board.

ON THE CAMPAIGN TRAIL

A WIN AND THE WORK AHEAD

My opposition to the anti-busing initiative helped propel me to a face-off in the general election against Doug Jewett, even though the polls showed the initiative was going to pass. All the other candidates continued to shun the discussion, but my tenacity was one reason I was moving on to the general election. But, would opposition to I-34 be a solid campaign strategy going forward? Some of my advisors were wondering if backing off the busing issue might be a better path for the general election.

At one of the first meetings of my steering committee, the topic came up. Field Director Sue Tupper remembers, "After the primary, they started including me in some of the steering committee meetings with Bob Gogerty, Walt Crowley, Jason King, Don Stark, Bob Watt, Greg Nickels, Tim Ceis, and campaign manager, Charles Rolland. At one meeting, someone suggested that Norm should back off the busing issue. I'll never forget. Gogerty let the discussion go on for only so long before he stepped up and brought his fist down on the table. He said Norm should not back off the busing issue, that if he did, he would no longer be who he is. In other words, let Norm be Norm. Bob settled that issue right there and then."[6]

Shortly after the primary, it was clear Initiative 34 was headed

32

for a victory in November. All the polling indicated the Initiative was going to win. An article in the *Seattle Times* just a few days after the primary outlined the importance of the busing issue in the upcoming campaign. "Seattle voters overwhelmingly oppose busing as a means of achieving racial balance in the city's public schools, and most support the anti-busing initiative aimed for the November ballot, a *Seattle Times* Poll indicates. Sixty-eight percent of those polled said they opposed mandatory busing, with 51 percent saying they are strongly opposed to it. Twenty-five percent favored busing, with only 5 percent saying they are strongly in favor of it. Eight percent are undecided...Busing and the quality of schools is emerging as the most important issue in the campaign for Seattle Mayor between City Attorney Doug Jewett and City Councilman Norm Rice. Half the polled voters said they would consider the candidates' stands on busing and education in deciding which to vote for—far more than any other issue and despite the fact that the mayor has no official authority over operation of the schools."[7]

So we knew the election was going to be close. For one thing, Jewett came out of the primary in first place. And, as you can see, support for I-34 was strong. We needed to figure out a way to make I-34 the focus without it, per se, being the issue. What I mean by that is that my issue needed to be "bringing the community together" rather than just flat out opposition to I-34. We needed to talk about it in a manner that let people know it was the divisiveness of the campaign surrounding I-34 that we were against, not just the measure itself. The I-34 debate was complicated and we need to bring it down to some basics. It was dividing the community, it was racially-charged, and we had to have a means to integrate our schools. If not busing, then what?

What can make our schools better for all our kids? I set out to make that the issue, not merely opposition to I-34.

I understood—and Constance, Bob Watt, and Bob Gogerty agreed—it was not enough just to oppose Initiative 34. We had to, and I wanted to, propose something positive in response to all the negativity surrounding the busing ban. Keep in mind that my main reason for running was to bring all sides to the table to heal the wounds caused by the debate. I hated what was happening in my city. This was the place Constance and I decided to stay and dig roots. We had long since been fixtures in the community by the time I launched my second run for Mayor. We were dedicated to public service, education, and the betterment of our city. We raised our son here and were deeply committed to Seattle and its citizens in a very profound way.

About two and a half weeks before the election, Doug Jewett and I had a debate where I-34 took center stage. That debate was held at Mt. Zion Baptist Church, where Constance and I were married. As the *Seattle Times* reported, "Seated at opposite ends of a 20-foot table, the mayoral candidates engaged in the most pitched debate of their 5-week-old general election campaign. Jewett wants to 'use $4 million in city money to keep Black kids on one side of the Ship Canal,' Rice charged.

Rice is evading the issue, 'speaking in platitudes' without accepting the fact that racial segregation 'is not the reality of Seattle in 1990,' Jewett said.

They glowered at each other, voices strained, interrupting each other while a moderator made like a referee at a boxing match. But it was only the volume and the intensity that were new—not the arguments. Since the opening salvos on primary night last month, the two have hardly wavered in their debate over schools and busing. Ironically, it is the one campaign issue the next mayor will have the least control over; schools are the exclusive authority of the Seattle School Board."[8]

Any time the main debate in an election is over something that brings out the worst in race relations and perceptions of each other, the conversation can turn nasty. The election was heating up and that was part of my point. Let me make it clear: Although I was accused in the media of flip-flopping on the busing issue, I never did. I was opposed to I-34 because it was tearing my community apart. I was opposed to I-34 because it did not offer solutions for desegregating schools or making schools in any part of the city any better. I thought there were arguments to be considered in favor of phasing out busing or ending it completely for younger children. But I was opposed to I-34 because it was divisive and didn't offer any solutions. No one was really arguing that segregation is a good thing. But if that is the result, then shouldn't we be doing everything in our power to promote desegregation? I thought so, and that's why I wanted to propose a way to reach a solution. Even though there wasn't universal support for the measure, I-34 would likely pass. Tim Egan in the *New York Times* described the situation, "Although polls show the initiative has wide support, both of the city's daily newspapers have been highly critical of the measure. Seattle city legal officials tried, unsuccessfully, to keep it off the November 7 ballot, challenging its validity in court. Some of Mr. Rice's supporters have accused Mr. Jewett of playing to racial fears, comparing his anti-busing campaign to the presidential election last year and George Bush's use of Willie Horton, a Black man who committed crimes after he was furloughed from a Massachusetts prison. In one heated exchange last week, Mr. Rice accused Mr. Jewett of 'wanting to keep Black kids on one side of town.' Mr. Jewett replied that 'busing has fostered segregated schools because so many whites have left the system.'"[9]

When I entered the general election in the fall of 1989, I wanted to offer voters a long term plan to eventually end mandatory busing, but it would need to be a plan that worked to integrate our schools, and not abandon the goal of desegregation. It wasn't my opposition to the anti-busing initiative that led me to win the general election. It was my call for a comprehensive, citywide education summit to address all the issues involving our schools. It seemed to have a calming effect on the tensions of the municipal election, almost as if people were breathing a sigh of relief, "Let Norman fix it."

The time frame between the primary and the general election was just over a month, so we had no time to waste in pulling our folks together and getting our voters out. We had come in second, after all, so we had some challenges ahead of us. We worked hard. I continued to oppose I-34, but I also proposed a small business and occupation tax increase in order to hire 100 new police officers in an attempt to stem the rising crime rate in the city. Public safety had always been a major issue for me because it's essential to quality of life. People have to feel safe in their communities and in their homes. And of course I felt a need to heal the scars of a wounded city after the busing debate. I knew that if I were to win this election, we would have some healing to do.

My crime proposal may well have ended up being more important to the voters than race or busing. I had the sense that growing fears over crime was foremost in the minds of the electorate and that fit with my vision of safe, healthy neighborhoods. It's hard for people to be active and involved members of the community if they are afraid in their own homes or going to the grocery store. So my crime proposal got a lot of coverage and a lot of support.

Charles Rolland and the team he had assembled to organize the Democratic caucuses in 1988 engaged and recruited people from that effort to participate in our 1989 campaign. Even though we had name familiarity and a strong position, we still needed the field operations, get out the vote expertise—and the Rainbow Coalition, together with Team Rice (folks who had worked on my previous campaigns), became our secret sauce. The coalition was instrumental in garnering primary endorsements or joint endorsements from groups outside the usual groups. And because we jumped into the race so late, most of the establishment endorsements had already been made. As Sue Tupper remembers, "When you got in, all the standard groups involved in doing endorsements, all that was done so we didn't have a choice but to put a different structure in place."[10] Bob Watt's added, "We had no endorsements, none at all compared to other people, which meant we were free to really listen to the people, not the unions, not the business people, I remember saying to myself that this is going to be a blessing."[11]

On November 7, I received 58 percent of the vote to Doug's 42 percent. In the end, we found ourselves with a Hobson's choice: the initiative passed—and I was elected mayor. In his article for the *New York Times,* Tim Egan reported what Charles Rolland noted about the historic significance of the victory, "We made history. The conventional wisdom has always been that a city needs to have at least 40 percent minorities to elect a Black mayor. We proved that wrong."[12]

The Black population in Seattle when I was elected was 10 percent so we felt very good about this win. Charles estimated that a considerable percent of voters who voted in favor I-34 also voted for me, which led to journalists and pundits saying the Seattle electorate had sent a mixed message. They were in favor of the first African-American mayor, but they were also in favor of an anti-busing initiative the African-American mayor-elect had opposed. In the end, the anti-busing initiative barely passed with only a one percent margin of victory. I won by 16 points so obviously, there was a lot of crossover voting.

Family and friends came from all over the country to celebrate our inauguration. There were activities throughout the week, culminating in parties all over the city. We had engraved souvenir champagne glasses with the inscription "Mayor Norm Rice, Jan. 5, 1990. Celebrate Seattle."

Oh, and celebrate we did! The *Seattle Times* reported on the inauguration party that Friday night at the Westin Hotel. "Rice was quick to credit Constance, who has a doctorate in education, for her support and accomplishments.

'In most circles, I'm Dr. Rice's husband. I ran for mayor so I would have a title.' Guests were quick to praise him and the event. As Municipal Judge Fred Bonner said, 'This is special. It's an event, a recognition of worth and dedication and competence.'"[13]

My brother, Otha, my mom, and her cousin, Dorothy, and my sister, Audrey, were all there to help me celebrate. My mother was also quoted in The *Seattle Times*. "Norman has always been successful in everything he's done. He's never been any trouble. He's always been good."

Well. That's what moms are for. It meant a great deal to me to have my mother there on that special night. In fact, all the strong women in my life were there to celebrate. It was a special night to celebrate and we partied. But we also knew we had a hell of a lot of work ahead of us.

Front: Norm Rice, Audrey Rice Oliver (sister),
Rev. Susie Rose Wittman (grandmother),
Irene H. Powell (mother) Constance W. Rice
Top: Otha Rice, Gerald Rice (brothers) Mian Rice (son)

PART II

BRINGING PEOPLE TOGETHER FOR EDUCATION

BUSING AND SEATTLE PUBLIC SCHOOLS

In order to provide context for the election and the education summit to come, it is important to understand the history of busing in Seattle. The landmark Supreme Court ruling *Brown vs. Board of Education* came down in 1954, the same month I turned eleven years old. However, the landmark decision did not spell out any method or specific timeline for ending racial segregation in schools. It only ordered states to desegregate "with all deliberate speed." I was approaching my thirties before the country really started dealing with integrating our public schools, which begs the question of what "with all deliberate speed" really meant. The ruling was one of the most significant advances of the civil rights movement because it dealt with equal opportunity for African American children in education.

Segregation of white and colored children in public schools has a detrimental effect upon the colored children. The impact is greater when it has the sanction of the law, for the policy of separating the races is usually interpreted as denoting the inferiority of the negro group. A sense of inferiority affects the motivation of a child to learn. Segregation with the sanction of the law, therefore, has a tendency to

retard the educational and mental development of
negro children and to deprive them of some of the
benefits they would receive in a racially integrated
school system."[14]

"'The African American struggle for desegregation,' observes
Gary Orfield, co-director at the Harvard Civil Rights Project and
among the nation's leading experts on desegregation, 'did not
arise because anyone believed that there was something magical
about sitting next to whites in a classroom. It was, however,
based on a belief that the dominant group would keep control
of the most successful schools and that the only way to get full
range of opportunities for a minority child was to get access to
those schools.'"[15]

By the early 1970s, cities were being ordered left and right
by federal courts to start busing children across their cities in
order to achieve racial integration. According to the Leadership
Conference on Civil Rights Education, "Enactment of the 1964
Civil Rights Act in response to the nonviolent civil rights movement finally spurred action. In 1966, the Fifth Circuit Court,
in *United States v. Jefferson County Board of Education*, ordered
school districts not only to end segregation but to 'undo the
harm' segregation had caused by racially balancing their schools
under federal guidelines. Jefferson was followed by the Supreme
Court's Green v. County School Board of New Kent County
decision in 1968, requiring desegregation plans that promised
to work right away.

A strong federal commitment to enforcement of the Civil
Rights Act of 1964 proved critical. In the first five years after
the Act's passage, with the federal government threatening
and sometimes using fund termination enforcement provisions
(i.e., cutting off federal funding to school districts that failed
to comply with the law), more substantial progress was made

toward desegregating schools than in the 10 years immediately following the Brown decision. In 1964, 1.2 percent of African American students in the South attended school with whites. By 1968, the figures had risen to 32 percent."[16]

Seattle's busing history was different from the rest of the nation's because Seattle was never under the thumb of the federal courts. Seattle wanted to deal with integration without federal court intervention and embarked on a decades long struggle to integrate its schools by busing students. Seattle's school choice system was struck down on constitutional grounds. According to the *Seattle Times*, "In the 1970s, Seattle was credited as the first big city to implement busing before being ordered to do so by a court. The district abandoned the practice two decades later, but it maintained a choice plan with a so-called racial tiebreaker, which gave assignment preference to students who could improve a school's racial balance. That policy was challenged in 2000 and found unconstitutional in 2007."[17]

The effort to integrate Seattle schools has now totally been abandoned with mixed results. Conservative courts, white flight, and several new challenges have all but ended busing to achieve racial integration. Despite the fact Seattle was forward looking enough to want to integrate its public schools before being rapped on the hands by some federal court, it was not socially evolved enough to stick with it and endure school busing. Even many in the liberal community in Seattle started sending their kids to private schools. We didn't experience the white flight to suburbia like most cities did, which I think has more to do with our topography. With natural boundaries like water and mountains limiting the actual land mass size of the city, where were Seattleites to flee? To private schools is where. White enrollment dropped precipitously during our busing-to-achieve-racial-integration efforts.

I supported busing and, although mistakes were made, it

likely would have continued and succeeded if we had done it right. Perhaps it would be more accurate to say I supported the lofty goals of busing because I always knew the separate but equal doctrine laid out in *Plessy v. Ferguson* could never be true for our country. The problem we had was that our neighbor-hoods would remain segregated no matter what we did with busing to integrate our schools. At the end of the day, students still returned to their neighborhoods like boxers back to their corners. We felt in the early days, busing might change all that. If students learned to live and work side by side then, naturally, they would learn to buy houses next door to each other. Per-haps if we had not abandoned busing, our neighborhoods would be more integrated to this day. In 2015, a thought-provoking article for the *Washington Post*, Syracuse University Professor, George Theoharis, says that it wasn't busing that failed; rather it was the country's resolve that failed. "Public radio's 'This American Life' reminded us of this reality in a two-part report in July of 2015 called 'The Problem We All Live With.' The program noted that, despite declarations that busing to deseg-regate schools failed in the 1970s and 1980s, that era actually saw significant improvement in educational equity. When the National Assessment of Educational Progress began in the early 1970s, there was a 53 point gap in reading scores between Black and white 17-year-olds. That chasm narrowed to 20 points by 1988. During that time, every region of the country except the Northeast saw steady gains in school integration. In the South in 1968, 78 percent of Black children attended schools with almost exclusively minority students; by 1988, only 24 percent did. In the West during that period, the figure declined from 51 percent to 29 percent."[18]

Seattle wanted to be a leader in the quest to desegregate schools, but for many citizens busing really wasn't any more popular in the Pacific Northwest than it was in the Deep South.

In fact, a lot of the opposition came from the African American community because it was, by and large, Black children who were taking the long bus rides to attend schools in the predominately white neighborhoods of North Seattle.

In her essay on the internet website, HistoryLink.org, Cassandra Tate explains the Seattle School district tried a couple of schemes to bring more racial balance to our classrooms, including measures that encouraged Black students to transfer out of their neighborhood schools into predominantly white schools and a magnet program intended to entice white students to attend predominantly Black schools. These measures had some limited success in the beginning, but, there was wide disagreement among civic groups and community leaders over how best to achieve racial balance. Some of those groups felt that in order to overcome years of ingrained patterns, more coercive policies would be needed. "Faced with the threat of further legal action from advocates of integration, the School Board took its first tentative steps toward mandatory busing on November 11, 1970, adopting a Middle School Desegregation Plan that involved busing about 2,000 middle school students."[19]

A lawsuit filed by an organization created to oppose busing, Citizens Against Mandatory Busing, put those plans on hold for two years. During that time the specter of federal intervention loomed large and civic rights groups were threatening to sue if Seattle did not come up with an integration plan. After the Washington State Supreme Court upheld mandatory busing in 1972, Seattle came up with a plan. "The School Board responded with what became known as the Seattle Plan, expanding the busing program to include all the schools in the district. The plan was approved by a vote of six to one on December 14, 1977. The action made Seattle the largest city in the United States to voluntarily undertake district-wide desegregation through mandatory busing."[20]

Seattle, remember, was the only major metropolitan area in the country in September of 1978 *not* ordered by a court to desegregate its public schools and the city was proud of that. According to Tate, "The Seattle Plan was launched on a wave of optimism and good intentions, with support from a broad coalition of political leaders and community groups, including the NAACP, the ACLU, The Urban League, The Chamber of Commerce, The Municipal League, The League of Women Voters, The Church Council of Greater Seattle, and both the outgoing and newly-elected mayors."[21]

The first anti-busing measure passed a mere six weeks later, indicating Seattle voters were not as enamored with the plan as public officials had hoped and now it was quickly falling out of favor. White flight to private schools was increasing and enrollments were plummeting. Citizens were fed up with the school system and were being asked to stop implementation of the busing plan that, just a few years earlier had been a source of bragging rights. Even though voters knew a repeal of busing would mean the loss of federal tax dollars, they were, nonetheless, being asked to stop busing as a means of integrating the public schools. But in 1982, the US Supreme Court ruled the anti-busing initiative was unconstitutional and thus the city's plan was again upheld.

Enrollment for white students had been declining in Seattle since 1960 but it wasn't just a preference for the suburbs that was causing the numbers to change. "It was also clear that some white parents were taking their children out of public schools in Seattle because they did not want them bused out of their neighborhoods. In the first year of district-wide busing, the number of white students dropped by nearly 12 percent compared to the previous year, reducing total enrollment by 10 percent. Both the percentage of white students and the overall number of students fell steadily during the years of mandatory busing."[22]

In June of 1989, the anti-busing Initiative 34 was launched, and it passed at the same time we won the mayoral election.

After we won the election, we knew the work ahead went far beyond the issue of busing students. It went to the heart of equality, racial divides, and the achievement gap (although we didn't call it that back then). I knew it was important to bring back that sense of community that has always been so apparent in Seattle. I had to help heal the wounds the debate over this initiative had caused, which had the potential to turn Seattle into a powder keg of resentment and distrust.

To end the contentiousness and racially charged rhetoric over the busing debate, I wanted to offer a mechanism that would allow entire neighborhoods to get involved in finding solutions. Remember, while I was opposed to I-34, the anti-busing initiative, I never really saw busing per se as the issue. My issue was the mean spiritedness of the thing. To me, it was perhaps more the way Seattleites were dealing with busing than busing itself. Busing, after all, is about equality of opportunity in education, so whatever we did, it had to involve the school system.

Despite the ugliness swirling around the debate, I knew we all shared the desire for good schools in every neighborhood. Getting to agreement on the shared value was easy. We wanted all children to have equal opportunities, to get a quality education, and we wanted diverse schools. But how do we get there?

The process had to be accessible to everyone in the city and, in the end, we needed buy-in from all stakeholders. I wanted everyone to have skin in the game, so that's what led to the idea of a citywide Education Summit. I started talking about it and including it in speeches and television ads.

STRONG COMMUNITIES
ARE THE KEY

When I was growing up in Denver, my mother was never more than a mile away from my school. If I needed her to be there, she was there. But with changing demographics, such as parents whose work takes them out of the neighborhood, and the influx of non-English speaking parents, comes the need for more support for families. As our world was changing, the schools needed to adapt and change as well. We needed to reassess the role of school in a child's life and in the community. And it was key to determine the kind of support parents require to help them do their best when it came to their relationship with education and their children's schools. My vision was a city all working together to provide services and support for our schools and families.

Once we committed to the Education Summit, I found myself mustering all the leadership qualities I felt I possessed to start to heal the wounds the debate over this initiative had caused, and the divisiveness that had been unleashed.

THE EDUCATION SUMMIT:
A Monumental Endeavor

Pulling together a divided community to talk about perhaps the most divisive issue the city had ever faced was an enormous undertaking, and we knew it. But those of us involved from the beginning had no idea it would be as large and successful as it was nor how much work it would be. With the passage of a total ban on busing to achieve racial integration, we needed real solutions that would bring the community together to turn Seattle Schools into high-performing educational institutions *for all children*. How exactly to do that was the question. Sue Tupper, who after the election became a Special Assistant to the Mayor in our administration, tells me at least I had a sense of humor in the face of so much work. "You were in that meeting (after the election) and we were talking about how to move forward on the Education Summit and you joked 'Are you sure I said 'summit? I think what I said was Education. And that's the sum of it.'" [23]

This was going to be months of hard work, but it was also going to be a labor of love. From the very beginning, the people involved in this effort were passionate about their city, extraordinarily talented in their fields, dedicated to education, and determined to make change. Sometimes when fighting the good fight, you have to stop and remember: Government at its best is simply people working to make their communities and the lives of their fellow citizens better.

THE PLANNING BEGINS

Bob Watt had already signed on to serve as deputy mayor and I'm thankful he was by my side, keeping the project on track, and working closely with everyone in the mayor's office, as well as every single city department. Bob was well aware of the obstacles that lay ahead, and his wisdom and guidance was crucial to the success of the summit. Bob and other summit organizers, all of whom were deeply connected to the community in one way or another, could feel the remnants of anger, fear, and resentment still floating around Seattle. The warring factions were strong and vocal, especially in the education community, and rebuilding trust would be our greatest challenge.

Mayoral intervention in urban education reform was a bold move for a first major initiative. Mayors are often hesitant to spend their political capital on public education since they do not appoint school board members and have no control over the school district's fiscal policy. But I felt mayoral leadership was needed to bring full engagement of the community to public education and to ensure school system accountability. And truly, an improving public school system is a key social indicator for urban livability and indeed community development—but there were turf battles going on and a lot of fear among different stakeholders. We knew our success would hinge on getting them all on board.

I told the people of Seattle I would bring together a fractured city and they put their faith in me. We needed to wrap our arms around public education and educational equity and get the community passionate about good schools and equal opportunity.

The first thing we did was call on community leaders, respected activists, and experts in their fields to help us coalesce around a plan. How we would get buy in, who would be involved, and how to pull it together was the great unknown.

SETTING THE AGENDA

Dr. Constance Williams Rice holds a graduate degree from the Evans School of Public Policy and Governance at the University of Washington, and a Ph.D. from the university's College of Education. So when we looked for leadership on the planning committee, my incredible wife was the first person we thought of. She agreed to co-chair the planning committee with KING5 Broadcasting head, Ancil Payne. By March of 1990, the committee, known as the Agenda Planning Committee, had already met four times, including subcommittee meetings. According to Constance, "It was a daunting task, but Norman had pulled together an incredible team for his mayoral campaign and we used that team to help mobilize for the Education Summit. It was a winning team and the summit was hugely successful."

Linda Thompson-Black, now the Director of the Pacific Northwest UNCF (United Negro College Fund) served as my Deputy Chief of Staff for Education in 1990. She was on the ground floor of the summit planning process and her outreach work with the committee and beyond was crucial to the success of the entire event. Remember, in tackling this issue, we were facing a hostile world, so it was critical to articulate exactly what we were planning to do and bring people along as we went. The make-up of the committee had to represent a broad spectrum of the city.

In a March 5 update to the planning committee, Linda Thompson-Black reported the extraordinary progress we were making in setting the design, format, and agenda of this effort "The purpose of the Education Summit is to move all segments of Seattle 'toward a comprehensive solution to the education problems facing our schools and community.' The Education Summit will seek to mobilize the broadest possible representation of Seattle leadership—business, union, religious, professional, civic, and most critical of all, teachers, parents, and students—in a discussion of education issues."[24]

"The planning group is composed of 60 individuals, representative of: parents; students; teachers; principals; school administrators; the superintendent; school board; state legislature; county council; city council; private schools; the governor; business; community organizations; multi-ethnic; high school; middle school; k-5, pre school; higher education; and other interests."[25]

UNPRECEDENTED OUTREACH:
Three Hundred Meetings

As the planning committee was being formed, Linda was already reaching out to the community. The committee intended to reach, represent, and enlist the broadest coalition possible to support the summit. To that end, Linda and her team went back to the committee repeatedly, which built their trust. As she describes it, "I know I had three hundred little meetings of all the factions before we got to the summit and I think that was key. The anti-busing initiative crowd was tough. I mean they were on our case and they were gonna have their say and it was a challenge but we did it with respect. We listened, we wrote it down, we sent it back to them, and they could see their voice was heard."[26]

Bringing this group of influential stakeholders together made us feel as though we had already made great progress because moving beyond the summit, the planning committee represented the folks who would be influential in implementing the policies and programs that would come out of it.

With input from Linda's outreach, the planning committee began with a list of the stakeholders' greatest fears regarding the summit's possible success or failure. It included fears that the summit would:

- Fail to include all elements within the community;

- Fail to create a strong action plan;

- Repeat past exercises, avoid dealing with the profile of students today, and fail to address the holistic needs of education;

- Focus on criticizing education by participants, become diffuse and lose commitment after the agenda-setting process;

- Fail to accomplish anything because of having too many items to address; and

- Fail to provide additional resources.

Keeping these fears in mind, along with their hopes for the

summit, the committee framed a statement titled Values and Preferred Outcomes. It began with trust, renewal, and healing:

- The summit should build trust between the major institutional players involved in education; community-wide organizations reflecting civic and business interests; groups reflecting the needs and desires of Seattle citizens; and individual citizens.

- The summit should result in a sense of community renewal built around a common focus of education.

- The summit process should help heal community rifts, *particularly* (but not exclusively) those which have developed around education issues.[27]

In a way, the committee had come full circle back to the point of mending the gapping tear in the community. We were on the right track.

The committee agreed Phase I of the summit would be two days of community-wide brainstorming sessions held all over the city. Linda Thompson-Black notes, "Discussions would occur in community centers, senior centers, and the meeting places of established community groups, in order to generate the most diverse participation possible and tap difficult-to-reach populations. Fieldworkers, translators, and other special efforts would be made to identify and include populations which do not speak English or do not tend to participate in community meetings."[28]

The need for a full-court press public information campaign was obvious. Walking our talk meant getting the biggest and broadest participation in any civic endeavor in the city's history. To do that, we had to tell the public exactly what we were doing, keep them apprised of the planning, and convince them to participate.

As we were building the coalition, building trust at this stage was important so people would stay involved all the way to action on the items the summit would identify. The planning committee really was made up of the folks who would be influential in implementing the solutions from the summit.

FROM PLANNING TO IMPLEMENTATION

The committee adopted the Education Summit Implementation Plan 1990. It asked the groups and individuals who participated to commit resources and to work together to achieve progress on three to five major education issues. The issues would be identified by the summit participants.

The Education Summit plans were taking shape. It was agreed the summit would consist of two sets of meetings.

- Education Weekend: April 21 and 22, would involve two days of simultaneous brainstorming sessions all over the city.

- Two Day-Summit: May 5 and 6 would serve to develop a consensus around the brainstorming sessions and a day of developing draft action plans to achieve those goals.

- Phase III of the Education Summit would utilize task forces on specific priority issues to flesh out the draft action plans, and secure commitments from "government, business, labor, the school district, and the broad community."[29]

The design of the summit was very deliberate. Tupper remembers that the first ideas for the summit were different from what ended up as the final format. "The first thinking began with how you would typically look at a summit: get the key players, all the voices involved from the various factions who had been engaged in the education issue at that point. Get them around a table in a setting where people could come and be in an audience and observe this discussion taking place. Well, it didn't take a rocket scientist to figure out that these had been the very people who were frankly part of the conflict and getting them to come to an agreement on their own was a bridge too far. We had to include those voices, but do it in a way that would not allow any one person or organization to hijack the whole thing."[30]

Public relations guru and friend, Laird Harris, agreed to head the Implementation Team now that the format for the summit had been established. "The charge was to involve as many people from the community as possible. This was to happen along with the discussions that were going on later. The question was how do we do meetings where it's not going to be the same 30 people going from meeting to meeting to meeting and dominating? So that was where we got the idea of having simultaneous meetings—we didn't have any notion there would be 26 of them."[31]

Once the logistical planning was done, we laser focused on getting people to the Education Summit. We used the same strategy to ramp up attendance at the summit as we had used to get the voters to the polls on Election Day. We knew the summit had to be well attended to be successful. To get citizens to come, Team Rice set out to repeat the field operation so instrumental in our win. As Laird noted, it wasn't as simple as putting out posters saying "Y'all Come."

Tupper outlined our three-pronged approach. "Mark Murray, the Press Secretary, was doing a really aggressive job of working the media, so we had that going on as a public wide invite. Linda had this crazy effort going on dealing with all those bazillion organizations and then having them get the word out through their membership. But to get just regular average citizens out of their homes on a Saturday, how do you do that? We put together a personal invitation letter from the mayor and the Team Rice people knocked on the doors of every single education levy voter in the city. They gave people this letter, this invitation from Norm, asking them to give up their time and come to the summit. I think that was a key piece to getting people (there.)"

The first stages of the summit took place on April 21 and 22, 1990, with what turned out to be a total of 32 neighborhood meetings. Mindy Cameron of the *Seattle Times* described what it was like, "Laird Harris was nervous. He had carefully reserved the Saturday noon hour to handle last minute problems. But here it was 12:30 and his biggest worry was sunshine.

He'd been hoping for clouds. The only last-minute glitch he could do anything about was the lack of cables at several sites around town. Extra cables had been dispatched.

Volunteers were fidgeting, checking lists, making phone calls. In a corner office of the 12th-floor executive complex at the Seattle Municipal building, Tom Tierney, Deputy Chief of Staff to Mayor Norm Rice, was feeding a bottle to his three-week-old son, Ian.

It was an appropriate scene: adults filled with nervous anticipation and in their midst, a tiny baby. Children and hope. That's what the Education Summit was all about."[32]

The use of trained facilitators for the summit discussions was key to keeping the meetings on track, making sure no one was able to dominate. As Laird Harris explained,

"We had all these groups meeting simultaneously with experienced facilitators. Each facilitator had the same plan. So, there were certain topics they would be all be discussing. Bob Watt added, "Each facilitator used the same method to be sure that every member of every group had an equal opportunity to speak and be heard. To demonstrate that their words were heard and captured, each group had a trained recorder who wrote down the words spoken by every participant on a large white pad and asked, 'Is this what you said?' If the speaker did not think the words were accurate, the recorder re-wrote them. Each group had another recorder who was typing the exact words into a laptop computer. This process built trust that nothing would be distorted or lost. By Sunday afternoon April 22, four thousand five hundred Seattle residents had participated in one of the Education Summit meetings. All the participants were respectful and thoughtfully focused on moving things forward in a positive way for the children and families of Seattle.

Most important of all, their words were captured in a visible, accurate way so participants could see that they had really been heard and taken seriously."[33]

Linda Thompson-Black also talked about the importance in those first 300 meetings of people in the same room together communicating with each other. She attributed part of the success of the education summit to those early face-to-face meetings.

PHASE II:
From Brainstorming to Priorities

Phase II was held on May 5 and 6 and almost two thousand residents turned out to give voice to their concerns and offer input into solutions for the public schools. This phase represented a chance to pull all the brainstorming together, prioritize solutions, gain consensus, and adopt a plan. Each table at the citywide summit meetings was asked to nominate two people from their table to represent them at the Phase II sessions. This is where we developed the plan of action going forward.

Bob Watt knew from the beginning that the summit was going to be a monumental task. But when time came to pull it all together, Bob said the stage for success was already set. "Part of the success of the Education Summit was that we had a very diverse team of people. We picked locations that would bring us a diverse group of people. We wanted voices that were also happy with what was going on, not just people who were distressed. We had good facilitators and organizers. None of us had really seen anything like it. I believe it was the last Sunday of the summit and we put up all the white papers and 'Safe, Healthy, and Ready to Learn' jumped off the pages. We were looking for something that would capture the totality of the summit and that was it."[34]

Safe, Healthy, and Ready to Learn. That became our rallying cry and it was a phrase the entire city could get behind. It synthesized what we all wanted for our children. And unlike education funding, academic requirements, etc., these were specific goals that could be addressed by the city. The city would make sure the students were safe, healthy, and ready to learn. The idea that in terms of a child's chances for success, the environment that surrounds the child is as important as their educational experience was one we championed.

In order to achieve the goal of making every child safe, healthy, and ready to learn, we needed funding for the proposals to get us there. So after studying the results of the summit and, having listened to the community, we proposed a tax levy to pay for the proposals we had developed. As the *Seattle Times* reported:

Seattle city officials plan to place on this fall's general-election ballot a seven- year, $57.4 million education levy. The money, $8.2 million a year, would beef up health care and social services in Seattle public schools, and allow the school district to devote scarce dollars to classroom education. Mayor Norm Rice is expected to outline the details of the package tomorrow. But sources at City Hall and the school district said it would include four elements:

Early childhood development for children 5 years old and younger. The city would spend about $2 million a year to underwrite some of the costs of the school district's Head Start program.

School-based family services. The city would spend about $2 million a year to put family support workers, or counselors, in nearly every elementary school in Seattle. The counselors, which work to stem the number of school dropouts, now operate in about 20 (or a third) of the schools.

Comprehensive health care. The city would spend nearly $3 million a year to place nurses and other health-care providers in all public schools. The district now pays most of that bill.

Out-of-school activities. The city would spend more than $1 million a year to provide recreational, tutoring, and mentoring programs in schools, libraries, or recreational centers for 'latch-key' students who otherwise would be unsupervised at home."[35]

ENGAGEMENT TO ACTION:
The Families and Education Levy

The Education Summit was successful by every measure. We'd taken a comprehensive approach and our work and thoughtfulness paid off. After bringing almost five thousand citizens together, we had a roadmap to improve our schools through efforts from every sector of the city. Early on, I went to all my city department heads and asked them to present plans for their department to contribute to the success of our schools. And the result was true innovation born from engagement. For example, Holly Miller, the Superintendent of the Seattle Department of Parks and Recreation at the time of the summit, talked about what that department would bring to the table. "We had a lot of ball fields and there were opportunities to partner with the schools for recreational activities. In that way, we could contribute to the health and well-being of the students."

Andrew Lofton, who was our deputy chief of staff, currently Executive Director of the Seattle Housing Authority, was involved in the Education Summit and talked about our leadership. "The thing that set this summit apart from other endeavors of this kind was that Norman was authentic in his desire to have real people—not just leaders—involved. He truly wanted to hear from the folks that were affected by this. Other politicians have talked about the importance of civic engagement, but when the summit happened under Norm's leadership, it had a different feel from other efforts. We were not just going through the same old thing. You really had the feeling that people would be heard."

Additional innovations came from various city departments. The Metro Transit Authority agreed to provide support in the form of free bus passes for school field trips. The business community pledged to finance and develop a training institute for school district personnel, principals, and teachers. The health department and local health providers agreed to develop a comprehensive student health care system. The State agreed to provide additional early childhood education funding. The Seattle Public Library agreed to work with school libraries to coordinate information, making textbooks and assigned reading available at city branch libraries.

All of that, in just two short months, translated to about a million more dollars in additional support for the schools coming from the city. The Education Summit had identified what the community wanted and once we set the goal as, "Safe, Healthy, and Ready to Learn," our focus turned to a funding proposal to implement our priorities. Thus, the Families and Education Levy was born—and we worked hard and gained enough support to get the it on the ballot.

Now the challenge was getting voters to approve an increase in their property taxes and that can be an uphill climb. We worked hard and gained enough support to get the Levy on the ballot.

We pulled together the same team that helped us organize and get the vote out in the general election in 1989 and get citizens to attend the summit. Sue Tupper became the campaign manager for the levy campaign. "Going into this campaign, I really did feel like we had the wind at our backs. We had run an astonishing campaign to get Norman elected. We had pulled together thousands of Seattle residents to participate in a community-wide education summit and we had identified real, concrete strategies to deal with the problems in our schools. It seemed like the easy part would be convincing the voters it was worthy of funding."

After all our hard work, if this tax levy failed, it would be a huge setback for the momentum we had gained during the summit. The crowds that turned out for the summit were impressive and it received a lot of positive press coverage. People were talking again about public education in a hopeful and optimistic way. But was Seattle invested enough to *pay* for the changes we had worked so hard to identify?

The FEL (Families and Education Levy) would raise approximately $8 million a year for those programs identified to get us to "Safe, Healthy, and Ready to Learn." It would mean a cost of about $23 per $100,000 of property valuation—a cost we thought residents could live with and support, as it was money that would truly make a difference. Residents were suffering from increasing property tax assessments, but I was confident the will to improve the schools was there and community confidence in the Education Summit was high. A breakdown of where some of the money would be spent was outlined in the *Seattle Times*.

For early childhood development, the city would spend $2.2 million a year to:

> Subsidize child care for about 400 low-income families and provide health, nutrition, and mental health services and staff training to community day-care sites.

Underwrite some of the costs for the district's Head Start and CAMPI pre- school programs, which serve 732 children.

Establish at least three family resource centers that would refer parents to literacy and job-training programs and provide services for families with pre school children."[36]

Talk to anyone involved in education reform and addressing the achievement gap and you will hear how important it is to focus efforts on families and neighborhoods, as well as reading, writing, and arithmetic. For that reason, there were many other programs covered under the levy. We have to understand what is going on within families in order to help children in difficult situations get to the point where they are ready to learn. So the levy included a range of issues, including the use of family support workers, dropout prevention, elementary school guidance counselors, and counselors for homeless children. These programs were identified as critical to narrowing the achievement gap and they were included in the Families and Education Levy.

The levy would allow us to fully underwrite school nurses and health care workers, and expand teenage health services by adding school based health clinics. We wanted to provide nurses and counseling to pregnant students and students who were already parents, and increase drug and alcohol abuse services. Those were just some of the plans where we felt funding was badly needed. And we stressed passing this levy would free up almost $2 million dollars of school district money, spent on programs like these, for actual classroom operations and learning-based programs.

So we were guardedly optimistic the levy would pass because so many people had been involved in the summit and were now fully engaged, but it was a property tax increase and that's not always an easy lift. Yet there were signs as early as October the Education Summit may have already had an effect on the perception of the public schools. It was a boost to have the support of both Seattle newspapers, the *Seattle Times* and the *Seattle Post-Intelligencer*. The *Seattle Times* wrote:

> Seattle public schools couldn't have turned the corner on a 12-year enrollment skid at a better time. The renewed faith in the city's schools should bolster the already strong case for Seattle's $59.6 million levy for education and families on the November 6 ballot. That faith was reflected in the October 1 enrollment count—the key one in determining annual state aid of about $3,400 per student. The 43,601 students in Seattle schools number 2,600 more than the same date a year ago. It is 3,401 more than the district projected in its budget.
>
> There always is some attrition between now and January or February, but even with that, the district should receive almost $9 million more than it expected from the state.
>
> Interest in schools generated by the summit had to be a factor. The hundreds who brought their ideas to summit workshops had a new share in their schools. Developing the seven-year city levy, which will add $35 a year to the property tax of a $150,000 home, was an exercise in good faith. It was the product of community consensus developed through the summit.
>
> The levy provides a variety of social services for families and children and frees up dollars the Seattle

School District can use for better education. Helping
children at an early age so they'll be better prepared
to enter school is a vital cornerstone of the measure.

Voters can keep the corner-turning momentum alive by sup-
porting the November 6, levy.[37]
The following goals guided the development of the Family
and Education Levy which became Proposition 1 on the
November 1990 ballot.

- Implement community priorities established through
  the Education Summit.

- Make children safe, healthy, and ready to learn.

- Support families and strengthen parent effectiveness as
  educational partners.

- Develop Community Schools.

- Build stronger partnerships between schools and com-
  munity-based agencies.

- Celebrate cultural diversity and promote equal learning
  opportunities.

- Free school district resources to improve classroom
  learning environments.

As can often happen when a city government works to
improve the state of a school district, there was opposition
from a school board that was concerned their power was being
usurped. But this levy was savvy in its efforts to relieve some of
the financial burden on the school district, and in essence, assist
the school board in its mission. The effort confirmed the role of
the city to assist in the well-being of its youngest constituents.

Support for the measure grew quickly and community leaders stepped up to the plate in the effort to get the measure passed. According to the *Seattle Times*, "'Seattle is a family in crisis. We've got to pull together and save it, now,' said Don Covey, president of UNICO investments. The Families and Education Levy would raise $8.5 million a year for seven years to help children and families cope better in school and in life. Though it sounds like yet another school levy, it's not. It was dreamed up at last spring's citywide Education Summit as a new way of attacking the problems faced by the school district, from outside."[38]

Like a school levy, it would be funded by a city property tax. Unlike a school levy, however, it is targeted to meet needs that often prevent children from functioning well in school. It would not provide any direct school funding, but by paying costs for programs such as school nurses, it would allow about $2.1 million to be redirected to priority educational needs.[39]

Our efforts and organizing skills paid off. On November 6, 1990, Seattle voters approved Proposition 1. The broad support for the levy was a testament to the will of the entire city. Even folks with no children in the school district voted in favor of the Families and Education Levy. Paula Brock in her column in the *Seattle Times* featured several of those residents who supported the levy.[40]

> Deborah Duke's two children are in private school, but she voted for Seattle's Family and Education Levy anyway. After a year of frustration in the Seattle School District, Duke says she remembers the decision to take her children out. "At the spring concert they were singing that Whitney Houston song 'I Believe the Children are our Future' and I was feeling like I was abandoning the cause. But it doesn't mean we don't want this problem solved. It will take more than the levy. But this might help."

George Allen is single and doesn't have children, yet he also cast a ballot of support. People such as Duke and Allen played pivotal roles in the success of Proposition 1, a $69.2 million package that will benefit mostly public-school children. Yet they are among the 86 percent of city voters who don't have children in the public schools, according to a *Seattle Times* poll.

Dan O'Donnell directed the levy campaign on Capitol Hill. Both his children are in a Catholic school. "It's like people sometimes work for charities," O'Donnell said. 'They don't always work for self-interest or payback, and it's not guilt. Maybe it's a sense of obligation. If you're fortunate, it's a way of giving something back."

Jim Metz lives on Bainbridge Island and commutes to work in the city. His daughter graduated from the island's high school in June. This fall, Metz directed the levy campaign in Queen Anne, Magnolia, and Ballard. 'The quality of the schools has a lot to do with economic development,' he said. "If employers can't be assured there's going to be an educated work force, they're not going to locate here. The economic health of the whole region depends on it.'" [41]

The support of these voters, coupled with Seattle's education and parent groups added up to a 57 percent approval of Proposition 1. A large portion of the community became reinvested in our public school system. That's not a landslide margin, but the win is significant given the region's anti-tax mood."[41]

A large portion of the community became reinvested in our public school system. The levy was originally approved by voters in 1990 and proved to be a major success in moving toward a goal of helping our children be safe, healthy, and ready to learn. The levy was approved again in 1997, 2005, 2011, and 2018. It now provides over $200 million dollars over seven years in additional resources for the schools.

PART III

LESSONS IN CIVIC ENGAGEMENT

OTHER AVENUES FOR ENGAGEMENT:
Downtown Revitalization

Watching the Families and Education Levy pass with such broad support was truly satisfying. In just two years we had gone from a city divided and full of angst and anger over its public schools to approval of a property tax hike that would allow us to implement the reforms we knew would work and the community wanted.

The Education Summit happened in the first year of my first term as mayor and while it fulfilled a campaign promise, it also led to real reforms in our public schools. But once the levy passed, there were other issues facing the city. Bob Watt talked about the commitment we made in the mayor's office on day one. "When we first came into office, we wrote a series of values and commitment statements as a team that was crucial to building trust. We came at this not in a cynical way, not in a political way, but in a values-based way. As an administration we all had agreed to the value statements and those commitments, and they were threaded all the way through to the summit. And that's what really made it possible to do the comprehensive plan, the urban village strategy, and downtown revitalization.

When I came into office, downtown Seattle was in a slump, to say the least. We were losing two major anchor stores: Fredrick

& Nelson and I. Magnin & Company. We were in danger of going the way of so many cities, where downtown cores morph into ghost towns after five o'clock and are sometimes dangerous, even in daylight. We needed drastic change and innovation to bring downtown Seattle back to what it once was: a vital and safe place for our workers and our families.

In HistoryLink.org, an internet encyclopedia of Washington state history, Mary T. Henry describes my role, "Rice also took aggressive steps to reverse the economic decline of Seattle's downtown area....Rice worked to acquire a a presence in downtown Seattle. Rice worked to acquire a $24.2 million federal loan guarantee for the private re-development of Westlake Center and conversion of the Frederick & Nelson building into Nordstrom's flagship store. He also supported a campaign, eventually successful, to re-open Pine Street to traffic as an additional incentive for Nordstrom's move."[42]

We all knew growth in Seattle would be steady in the coming years, although I doubt any of us foresaw the phenomenal rate occurring now. But we knew growth was coming because Seattle already had a fairly strong business climate. Low taxes, high quality of life, temperate weather, and a massive high tech boom all contributed to the moderate to high growth we experienced in the early 1990s.

We had recently committed to solving our educational system woes, which is always good for economic development, and we were sprucing up our downtown core. Combine those efforts with the fact that we live in one of the most beautiful cities on the planet and we were bound to experience a boom in the coming years.

All that growth needed strategic planning and careful management. I wanted to make sure we were on top of it because without proper planning, growth can be a disaster. Seattle is very much a city of distinct and unique neighborhoods and the character of each neighborhood needed to be enhanced, not damaged by the ever-expanding work force. I wanted to make sure all growth management and urban planning was sensitive to the needs of each of our unique neighborhoods, not just accommodating growth at the expense of some. Again, this needed to involve the citizenry and, as with education, it was important for us to engage the city and involve our neighborhoods.

In their book about community development, authors Donna Fabiani and Terry F. Buss noted one of my biggest concerns. "Rice believed the mechanisms for most growth management and land use debates in Seattle were not inclusive of all citizens' views and did not reflect their hopes and fears for the future of their neighborhoods and the city. Instead, debates focused on technical and legalistic aspects of land use that required a sophisticated level of expertise in order to participate effectively. This and other obstacles to participation were what Rice intended to ameliorate during his administration."[43]

I prided myself on picking quality, talented, and committed individuals who shared my vision for the city and my dedication to inclusive government that brought with it community support. That meant having the good sense to ask Bob Watt to serve as my deputy mayor as soon as I was sworn in. Most people who know Bob describe him as quiet and steady, possessing an air of confidence and dedication that allows him to move people to action. As we discussed, Bob was instrumental in crafting a series of values statements we used to guide all our decisions. One such statement, a citizen involvement mission statement, would guide our actions on all issues, not just education. "To provide honest, accessible leadership and outstanding service to the citizens, employees, and regional neighbors of the City of Seattle, and further develop a clear collective sense of vision, empowerment, and responsibility. In order to make our diverse City and the surrounding region an even better place to live, learn, work, and play."

That mission statement served to guide us in all efforts to improve life in our great city. My eleven years as a council member solidified what were already strong relationships in the community. I knew tackling the issues ahead meant I would have to build on those relationships while developing new alliances at the same time.

In the first few months of my first term, I started meeting with officials of neighboring communities to talk about growth and planning for the entire area. I was a proponent of making our urban area strong and dense and reducing rural sprawl. If all your growth is too far outside the city, then transportation issues get worse as people move farther and farther away from their jobs. We are seeing that problem currently as Seattle becomes less and less affordable. If people can live, work, and learn close to home, they have more time to play and it increases their quality of life. We had opportunities then that may not exist anymore because the growth has been so explosive in the last five years. But in the early 1990s, we still had some breathing room in terms of growth management and planning and I believe we laid the groundwork for the philosophy that guides growth decisions to this day in many cities.

Before I became mayor, the city was working on a comprehensive growth plan that I never really liked. I felt it was lacking several major components. As Donna Fabiani and Terry F. Buss further discussed, "Rice wanted the Comprehensive Plan to be designed around core principles valued by the public and a planning framework designed around those principles that would guide development to meet Seattle's 20-year growth targets. As with the Education Summit, Rice wanted to distill these core principles before planning began so he tasked Gary Lawrence, former City Administrator of Redmond, to ascertain these principles through another citywide engagement process. Rice wanted an inclusive and broad engagement that did not just involve the usual planning activists. So the discussions were framed in human terms all people could relate to by being focused on people's hopes, dreams, and fears for the future of their neighborhoods and city. This was a change from previous planning debates that only focused on pro-growth vs. anti-growth."[44]

We enlisted the help of consultants DeLaunay and Phillips Inc. to bring together the Seattle Planning Commission and the Planning Department staff to conduct focus groups. The idea and our goal was to approach growth planning and management the same way we approached the Education Summit, with various focus groups and people from all walks of life participating.

A major component of our growth plan was the revitalization of downtown Seattle. Needless to say, downtown Seattle was a very different place 25 years ago. What is now one of the most vibrant, walkable, safe, and thriving downtown cores, once resembled a downtown right out of a film noir mystery. Frederick & Nelson, for years the most prominent and vibrant department store in the city, was closing and other businesses were following suit. When you walk downtown now, it's hard to imagine what it was like in the early 1990s. Drugs and gangs were common. We needed drastic steps to reverse the trend and that's what we did.

In the 1980s, the city had approved closing Pine Street to connect the downtown with Westlake Center. While that was seen as a way to make downtown more appealing to shoppers, in just a few years it had pretty much done the opposite. It was actually an impediment to shoppers instead of the draw it was designed to be. A lack of accessible parking was a serious issue that made shopping and working downtown a hassle and unpleasant.

On May 31, 1992, Frederick & Nelson—one of Seattle's

premier department stores that had first opened in 1918—shut its doors. For many residents, it was more than losing a store; it was losing a part of Seattle's history. There are generations of Seattle residents who remember their family trips each holiday season to Frederick & Nelson on the corner of Fifth Avenue and Pine Street. Nicole Brodeur, columnist of the *Seattle Times*, did not arrive in Seattle until 1998, but many of her readers made her wish she had arrived sooner to experience the legendary store. In her 2016 column, "The Beloved Frederick & Nelson: Reader memories and throwback photos," Brodeur shares some of Seattle residents' recollections. "Norine Anderson recalled a postcard that showed the store in all its Christmas glory. 'The message, as I recall (it's been a long time): Christmas is not Christmas without a visit to Frederick & Nelson,' Anderson wrote. One of the best notes came from Jane Pugel, 'a nostalgic old lady who misses that store, even as (she) shops online.' She wrote of taking the old No.10 bus from her home in Mount Baker with her small kids in tow 'to the very door of Frederick's.' She would get a haircut, shop for sewing supplies, new china, socks for her husband, clothes, shoes, sheets, Frango mints. 'Whatever I needed or longed for,' she wrote, 'it was at Frederick's.'"

I wanted to bring back that kind of joyful experience to those visiting downtown Seattle once again. A group of developers had already devised a plan for the old Frederick & Nelson site. It was a massive, three-block development and although there were skeptics and opponents, that plan and the subsequent steps we took under my administration are largely credited with a downtown revitalization. Our accomplishment has made Seattle the envy of many other cities. A recently released case study by the Pine Street Group examined the plan."

In 1993 (Developer Jeff) Rhodes began talking to Seattle's

business and government leaders about creating an upscale retail center on three downtown blocks that included the empty Frederick & Nelson building. Encouraged by the prospects, Rhodes partnered in 1994 with local Seattle developer Matt Griffin to pursue the project as Pine Street Associates (PSA), later to become Pine Street Development (PSD). Rhodes also brought in two former UIDC colleagues, Tom Klutznick and Ken Himmel, to assist with the project."[45]

The project depended on Nordstrom, a retail powerhouse, agreeing to build a new flagship store that would be connected to the retail center and thus, serve as the anchor store for the development. In order for them to agree to that, however, Nordstrom insisted Pine Street be reopened to traffic. It was a massive plan that I saw immediately as a cornerstone to revitalization. "The plan was audacious. They proposed buying the old Frederick & Nelson building and swapping it to Nordstrom for

Nordstrom's smaller department store on Fifth between Pine and Pike. Pine Street Association would buy and clear one block to build a retail center. When Nordstrom relocated to the old Frederick & Nelson space, the developer would convert the former Nordstrom into a mixed-use retail and office building. The Seaboard Building would ultimately be renovated to provide 60,000 square feet of office space on the lower levels and 24 condominiums above."[46]

In describing the negotiations, Bob Watt recalls, "My job was to make it all come together behind the scenes. The people who deserve mention, but don't often get it, are Mark Sidran and Jack Johnson, who were extremely helpful from the moment that Bill Bain and Jeff Rhodes walked out of my office. It was those two, plus other law department colleagues, who I am sure, enabled the whole process to be legal."

Reopening Pine Street between Fourth and Fifth Avenues was central to the plan, and we enlisted the help of Pine Street Association and the Downtown Seattle Association to convince voters it was integral to our vision for downtown. The voters came through once again when it was put to a vote in late 1995. But despite that vote, there were still skeptics about the project. A group of advocates for the homeless felt any money going to downtown needed to be spent only on low-income housing and anti-poverty programs. But I knew then that rebuilding our retail core would have a great impact, and that has proven to be true as the city moves forward. The economic impact of that one three block development is still being felt and, in my mind, has contributed greatly to Seattle being the thriving, growing international city it has become.

As the Pine Street Group wrote, "Despite the post-recession challenges, there is widespread agreement that the city's involvement with the Pacific Place garage has been a huge net positive. Norm Rice and the City Council were proven correct in believing that revitalizing retail in Seattle's core would benefit the entire community."[47]

Part of the negotiation on this development was that the city would retain control and own the parking garage underneath Pacific Place. That was a huge lightening rod for protest when we first offered the proposal, especially since the city was going to pay more for the garage than its appraised value. But we knew that if this development turned out to be the success we all believed it would be, we would more than get our money back when it came time to sell. And that has now proven to be The City, which paid $50 Million for the construction of the garage, later sold it for $87 Million. Not a bad return on our initial investment.

Although not all our efforts to plan and manage growth were embraced at the time, this one was. After I left office, as growth skyrocketed and the downtown core remained a vibrant, exciting,

and livable place, most of what we envisioned in my two terms as mayor has come to pass. I was strongly in favor of the development of the South Lake Union area, and that was accomplished early in the following decade. Until recently, you could not go downtown without encountering cranes and building sites and signs touting the latest development of housing and retail enterprises. It can all be traced back to the development of that three-block area and the re-opening of Pine Street.

The city now faces new challenges that cry out for our type of civic engagement. We need to, once again, engage the community on issues of the achievement gap, affordable housing, homelessness, police reform, transportation, and growth. If ever there was a time to re-introduce civic engagement, if we are going to preserve our fragile middle class and curb the rising tide of homelessness—that time is now. No one wants Seattle to become a city of the uber-rich and the homeless with no one in between. During my administration, we dealt with education, growth management, downtown revitalization, and economic development by bringing together citizens with community leaders, experts, and public officials to foster a sense of grassroots involvement. I believe using our model can help the city move forward with meaningful planning for years to come in any economic climate, no matter what serious challenges lie ahead.

RE-EXAMINING THE MODEL:
Engagement As Learning

As we face these politically turbulent times, polarization, cynicism, disillusionment, lack of civility, and other social and political forces inhibit our ability to find shared values. That inhibits the development of creative solutions to complex public policy issues because you have to find agreement on shared values. Framing questions around values first, with issues second, allows for building common ground and lessening the divisiveness prevalent in today's toxic political environment.

With the advent of social media and interactive technology, the possibilities for civic engagement become almost endless. I'm old school and think there's a lot to be gained from actual face-to-face interaction, but that's not always possible. We should learn to use technology in new and innovative ways in order to involve the largest possible number of citizens.

It might be easy to assume our model of civic engagement worked so well with the Education Summit because education is primarily a local issue of utmost importance for so many people. But other issues can be successfully examined through the lens of active civic engagement. This model can be used for all issues that confront us, whether it's health care, policing and public safety, taxation, growth, affordable housing, or homelessness.

Civic Engagement should be seen from the outset as a learning experience. If there is a problem in the community, then it makes sense to deduce something went wrong— something we did before or believed before—no longer works or makes sense. As a community, we have to figure out *what* went wrong and not *who* went wrong. We have to be serious about civic engagement as a learning experience, and not a blaming experience. Keeping blame out of the equation leads to more constructive civic dialogue. I outlined some of these best principles in an interview with Anne Miano of the Washington Technology Industry Association: Everything can't be about winning—it's about learning, talking about failure, and figuring out what to do differently. If you can make an honest assessment of what went wrong, you can grow. But if you focus on what 'they' did, you never move forward.[48]

If you want enthusiastic public participation in governing, it is imperative to provide your citizens a safe environment to express themselves. I have often said a lost voice is a lost cause and I believe that. If we are ever going to solve the problems facing our communities, it is imperative to promote dialogue over demagoguery. I know it sounds simplistic, but there have to be rules for civil engagement. Providing a safe environment for dialogue is key.

Hearing many diverse opinions and suggestions was paramount to the success of the Education Summit. People were able to express their views without ridicule or harassment or, worse yet, violence. We wanted to hear from a diversity of viewpoints. Too often politicians try to solve problems by hearing from only one side of the issue. It might be good for holding on to power, but it is a terrible way to govern.

While the idea for the Education Summit evolved from my concerns over anti-busing rhetoric, busing was most certainly not the focus of the Summit. Rather, the discrepancy in academic success rates of African-American students compared to their white counterparts was the real issue we all wanted to address. Busing was a lightning rod, but when the storm clouds of angry rhetoric are gone, what's left is the basic fact African-American students were not getting what they needed to succeed at the same rate as white students in the district. Why was that and how could we correct it? We were talking about the achievement gap. Once we could take an objective look at the achievement gap, and all the issues it encompasses, including where the children were going to school, then we could begin to identify solutions.

As with any complex issue in society, our world is multi-dimensional, our problems are multi-dimensional, and our solutions have to be multi-dimensional. The achievement gap has always had many components. If we were to address the issue of children succeeding, it meant their families had to succeed as well. How do we make life easier for parents working long hard hours and struggling to make ends meet while trying to help their children live full and active lives outside of school? How do we reduce dropout rates? How do we ensure our students all have access to quality education? All those issues and several dozen more became a part of the discussion. What could city departments do to help? It was all part of the Education Summit.

If you are successful in bringing together a diverse group of people with diverse opinions to solve problems, you learn very quickly people want to know that you heard them. It's often times more important than actually solving the problem their way. It takes patience to develop what I call "authentic listening" skills, but it is crucial for successful engagement. You have to have a real ear for hearing what people are actually saying, not just what you want to hear. And your reactions have to be authentic and responsive to what people are telling you. You cannot be thinking about your response until you hear them out. It is imperative facilitators develop these skills. No one should ever be elected to public office without the ability to hear what the folks who elected them have to say. The idea that any law-maker would have people thrown out of their offices or refuse to see people who did not vote for them is crazy and shouldn't be tolerated in a democracy. Once you've heard what someone is telling you, then you need to ask questions to eliminate any ambiguity about what they said. "Is that what you said?" should be a mantra for everyone leading civic engagement.

THE NEXT STEPS:
What Are the Solutions and
How Do We Get There?

Once you reach consensus on the issues and priorities you want to address, you need to identify the "what." The "what" in this sense refers not to the problem, because you've already identified that. This is the "what is your solution" question. What do you do, for example, to solve educational inequality? For the Education Summit, our "what" was "Safe, Healthy, and Ready to Learn." That's what we wanted for all our children. We wanted them safe: safe at home, safe outside, safe at school. We wanted them healthy in mind and body. Conquering the first two, we believed, was the best way to reach the third goal. So we put our goals first, and then began to tackle the solutions we could reasonably accomplish to get where we wanted to be.

It takes time to identify where your best solutions lie, and it's important to remember citizens must have input on the solutions, as well as identify the problems. So "safe, healthy, and ready to learn" came out of the Education Summit as our goal. Identify the "what" and you are ready for a discussion of the how. In terms of the Education Summit, we first had to figure out how to keep all children safe. A part of that is aggressively mounting interventions for children at risk, whether the risk came from a family member or a bully at school. All the issues involved in keeping our children safe were a part of how we moved forward. It was the same with ensuring our children were healthy.

We had the specific goals. We had input from all the stakeholders and we were very confident we had identified solutions in those measures the city could take to improve the schools. Keep in mind that while the schools were not directly under city control, we had identified ways in which the City of Seattle could make a positive impact on the operation of the schools. We could fund programs that were perhaps considered ancillary to education in the past, but our community had identified as a way to improve educational opportunity for children being left behind. As I noted earlier, I asked the heads of every city department what they could do to help our students and families in their pursuit of quality education. It involved departments throughout the city, such as parks and recreation, transportation, and health. This type of innovation and leadership is critical in the next aspect of civic engagement: ongoing dedication to the issue.

The Education Summit had to be more than just a collection of gatherings where people talked about solutions and then went their own way. At the outset of civic engagement on any issue, you must have a commitment from everyone involved that they will be in it for the long haul. As the solutions you have identified become a reality, then other, differently directed solutions will arise and there has to be a commitment to meet challenges as they crop up. We had the Families and Education Levy to hold our feet to the fire. When you ask voters to increase their taxes, you have an obligation to make sure those taxes are used well.

Once we identified Safe, Healthy, and Ready to Learn as the goals, obviously the next step was to figure out how to get there. We had identified things that were not working for our families and students. We knew they needed additional support and we had identified areas the needed new innovation. But how do we get there? The city does not run the schools and we could not affect certain issues like class size that were a function of the state. But all city departments could do something. The parks department could provide space, and the transportation department could use the bus system to provide support. We identified programs that the city definitely could offer that would help families ensure their children were safe, healthy, and read to learn. But how to pay for them?

The Families and Education Levy was our "how." Of course, when solutions need money, and they invariably do, it becomes even more imperative to have buy-in from the citizens. Doesn't it make sense that when you ask people to pay for something, they like what it is you're asking them to pay for?

ONGOING SUPPORT

In successful civic engagement, it's imperative for stakeholders to know they are in it for the long haul. Successful civic engagement requires stakeholders to commit to implement, support, and evaluate solutions from inception to execution. For example, if the city transportation department offers student passes allowing them to ride the bus for free, there has to be analysis of how much that costs, what the usage rate is, what kind of ongoing financial and logistical support is needed to continue that service. So when we asked our city departments what they could contribute to "Safe, Healthy, and Ready to Learn," we wanted to see long-range plans. We had to offer options that not only worked, but would be feasible to continue for years to come. There can be no ambiguity here. You need to be clear with all stakeholders, experts and citizens alike, there is an ongoing commitment to success. Once you have established what the community needs to do and what your goals are, then everyone has to commit to building it.

An ongoing commitment to a community project or issue is one of the most positive aspects and most rewarding outcomes of civic engagement. It means citizens will feel like they have built something, not just influenced policy, and more will support it. Citizens will be proud of having built sustainable solutions for their community—which is what successful civic engagement looks like.

AN EXAMPLE OF ENGAGEMENT:
Using the Model to Address Homelessness

Homelessness, like education, is again a multi-dimensional problem requiring a multi-dimensional approach. Let's examine how the model for the Education Summit might work for this issue. What would a Homelessness Summit look like?

The planning stage of any civic engagement project is critical. The first thing leaders need to do is pull together a group of individuals who are committed to examining all sides of an issue and who do not have a personal agenda other than solutions. As I described for the Education Summit, I began with a planning committee headed by Dr. Constance Rice and Ancil Payne. Constance is an expert in the field of education and Payne was expert in civic leadership. Together, they pulled in voices from all over the city to construct the summit. They provided a framework in the mission statement, and the planning took off. I was blessed with a dynamic team that understood the intricacies involved in planning such a huge undertaking and I asked that team to formulate the plan. Where will citizens meet? How will you get the word out? What topics will be addressed? What will citizen input look like? Who will lead discussions? These are just a few of the questions that we had to answer, and will need to be answered for any similar effort.

The Education Summit involved a series of meetings all over the city held on two separate days. A summit on homelessness could look very much the same. It would include experts on housing, public health, mental health, addiction, law enforcement, and crisis counseling. It would bring together homeless advocates, neighborhood activists, civil liberties experts, and addiction treatment specialists. It would be critical to provide facilitators, childcare, technical support, and hold meetings in convenient locations with parking and easily accessed by public transportation.

Because we were so successful with the model we used for the Education Summit, I tend to usually rely on that model in developing civic engagement projects and ideas. As long as the basic principles stay the same, technology can be used to develop new ways of bringing people into the conversation. But in the desire to use technology in this way, we cannot forget the power of face-to-face contact—eyeball-to-eyeball discussions. Let technology be a tool when needed, not the star of engagement.

SHARED VALUES AND
IDENTIFYING STAKEHOLDERS

You have to give people a pretty good reason to leave the comfort of their homes to change their Saturday afternoon plans. Instead of attending their child's soccer game or tackling the household chores they'd planned, you're asking them to sit inside for hours talking about homelessness. People will show up for all different kinds of reasons, but you have to start with shared values as a community. In the Education Summit, it was the shared desire to educate our children and to make sure they all have the same opportunities for success. Of course, some folks turned up because they were angry over busing, but coming together over the shared value of wanting all children to have the opportunity to learn encompassed all those ancillary issues.

When dealing with homelessness, what are our shared values? I don't like the use of the word "brand" but it's almost the same concept. This is where a strategic planning committee can begin. For our purposes, let's say our shared value is: shelter is a basic human need, people die without it, and we do not want people to die because they do not have shelter. People can pretty much universally agree people shouldn't die in America because they do not have shelter.

In pulling together the community, you have to identify

those people who are most invested in finding solutions. On the issue of homelessness, the list of stakeholders would naturally include neighborhood activists and business owners who don't want tents on their sidewalks, social workers who work with the homeless population, and public health officials, including addiction specialists and mental health experts. But it should go beyond that. For the Education Summit, we went to each city department and directed them to bring ideas their agencies could implement to benefit Seattle Public Schools. The same type of approach could be used for homelessness. Business leaders could offer much more than just complaining about tents if they banded together to provide job training or internships. In Seattle, we have organizations that do exactly that. One trains homeless residents (and yes, they are residents) to work in all capacities of the restaurant industry. Another, Real Change, a newspaper published and sold by homeless people is working to give the homeless population not only jobs, but also a platform for the discussion of matters that affect them. "Real Change exists to provide opportunity and a voice for low-income and homeless people while taking action for economic, social, and racial justice."[49]

There are more industries that could provide programs for the homeless and innovative leaders in the community need to be a part of the discussion. Other extraordinary innovations need to be developed or expanded, such as mobile health clinics, mental health treatment centers, and tiny houses that can provide a safe alternative to tents, to name just a few.

The discussion around finding solutions to homelessness will be contentious and difficult because of the nature of the problem itself. Solutions to homelessness are going to violate *someone's* space. Planners, stakeholders, and experts need to be prepared for much more than just the NIMBY (Not in My Backyard) crowd. They need to be ready for views that range from straight out wanting to build government housing to those who want to buy one-way bus tickets. There will be voices blaming crime and public nuisance problems—rightly or not—on the homeless population. So any civic engagement project on the issue of homelessness needs trained facilitators who are ready for all manner of arguments, temperaments, and opinions about not only the issue but the very people who find themselves in these circumstances. It will be important not to let any civic engagement on this issue rob this population of their humanity. That is the one thing that always gets lost in a discussion about homelessness, and leaders need to be careful not to let that happen. Remember, whatever solutions you arrive at, they will affect people's lives. The rhetoric now can be pretty ugly, and we need to use professionals to lead us away from that ditch.

What should guide any work is the actual public input and engagement itself. Remember, it is the job of our elected leaders to listen to what their constituents have to say, not find solutions and drop them from the mountain top.

After pulling together a group of experts to plan what engagement on the topic of homelessness might look like, it's time to bring in the community. In education, that meant parents, teachers, administrators, public health officials, counselors, family advocates, and others. On the issue of homelessness, that might include some of the same people. One extra benefit from productive civic engagement is that citizens begin to realize how closely the issues we face are connected. Education, homelessness, crime, addiction, taxation, government spending—they are all related to each other.

A ROADMAP FOR ENGAGEMENT:
A Matter of Trust

My advice to anyone thinking about seeking public office is to recognize the fundamental and critical role civic engagement plays in our democracy. Citizen involvement is the very heart of a participatory democracy. It's a matter of trust, folks. Civic engagement instills public faith in policy. For democracy to survive, the general populace has to believe those who govern have their backs.

In the past two or three decades, public trust has been waning. The Pew Research Center recently published Public Trust in Government: 1958-2017, a study of attitudes spanning almost 60 years. What they found was, while attitudes fluctuate, trust in government is way down. "When the National Election Study began asking about trust in government in 1958, about three-quarters of Americans trusted the federal government to do the right thing almost always or most of the time. Trust in government began eroding during the 1960s, amid the escalation of the Vietnam War, and the decline continued in the 1970s with the Watergate scandal and worsening economic struggles. Confidence in government recovered in the mid-1980s before falling again the mid-1990s. But as the economy grew in the late 1990s, so too did confidence in government. Public trust reached a three-decade high shortly after the 9/11 terrorist attacks, but declined quickly thereafter. Since 2007, the share saying they can trust the government always or most of the time has not surpassed 30%."[50]

When only a third of the population trusts the government *they themselves have chosen,* there is something seriously wrong, and it presents a clear and present danger to our democracy. People who don't trust government shut down. They don't vote, they don't attend public hearings, and they don't participate. For a democracy—that's deadly. So the first place we have to go is restoring public confidence in those we select to govern.

DUTY TO RESTORE TRUST

The issue of confidence in our politicians is a thorny one because it includes so many aspects. It may seem obvious, but we need to remind the people who govern that they are the ones we have *chosen* to govern. Citizens are the employers and public servants are the employees. Therefore, the people you have "hired" to take the reins of government have an obligation to listen to you, the employer. Our common ground should be that our government is composed of the people we picked to run it, and elected officials need to once again know the citizenry is their employer. And when your elected officials forget this, you have a duty to remind them who they work for.

It would be nice if trust in our elected officials was restored just by virtue of voters liking them and the way they govern. But the citizenry has to have a basic level of knowledge about government in order to have faith in it. People do not trust what they do not know. That's why civic engagement is such a great tool to restore trust; it teaches people about policy, about governing, and about compromise. But before we attempt civic engagement on any level, we have to recognize the importance education plays in instilling confidence in government.

We laugh when late night television presents "person on the

street" interviews with basic questions about government and history, and people give ridiculous answers. Think about that. It's not really funny. Ignorance is the enemy of a democratic society and we'd better get about the business of teaching our children how we govern in a democracy. Every child ought to learn early about the importance of voting, about what the various political parties believe in, the names of our past elected officials, and how local, state, and national governments operate. In this day and age we need to go way beyond basic civics and teach our students critical thinking skills. All our citizens need a solid educational foundation in the fundamentals of democracy and the importance of engagement.

Until our schools catch up in this regard, knowledge needs to come from government itself. Our leaders have an obligation to keep the public informed about what they're doing. After all, you have a right to know if your taxes are going up or your schools are closing down, or your electric bill is rising. You have an obligation to know when to put your trash out, when to avoid open fires, when to renew your car license tabs, how to license your pet. It's a constant give and take. Public officials have a duty to inform you about what they are doing, and you have an obligation to know what part you play.

LEARNING THROUGH THE
PRESS IS NOT A PLAN

I have never been a vociferous critic of the press. I had issues sometimes when I felt the coverage was unfair or inaccurate, but for the
most part when I was mayor, the press was honest, hardworking,
and most importantly, wanted to inform and educate their readers.
For those of us who grew up in the '50s, '60s, and '70s, we learned
our civics lesson watching Walter Cronkite on a black and white
TV. We learned about wars and why our leaders wanted to fight
them. We learned about the arguments against those wars, and
white America outside the South learned about civil rights.

But these days, you would be hard pressed to find national
media, especially cable television, engaged in much beyond what
I call horse race reporting: who wins, who loses, who is down in
the polls, who is up in the polls. Sometimes it seems that the
only reporting on issues like health care, voting rights, and civil
rights is made up entirely of who said what and who's got more
support, instead of details about what any proposal or measure
actually does. Excuse me, but I want to know what a law does
and how it affects my life, not whether it's better for one politician over another. Seriously. I hope sanity will be restored to the
national media and there will again be meaningful discussions
over policy, not who's winning the race.

A NOBLE PURSUIT

Public service is a noble pursuit and it should be treated as such. It might be good to abandon the word "politician" altogether as a way to describe our public servants because undoing years of mistrusting government starts with the people who make up government. Often, public servants give up more lucrative salaries to work in the public sector. Cities need to provide every opportunity for people to meet their public servants, both elected and appointed. If your friends and neighbors trust their city council member, even if they don't always agree with him or her, they are much more likely to engage when that council member calls on them.

We have to start coming from a place where instead of being the enemy or evil incarnate, we view government as what it is in this country: people getting together and deciding through debate, innovation, and compromise how they will govern themselves. We need to address this idea that government is the boogeyman. We need to remember government in this country is us; *by the people, for the people* is not just a slogan, folks. If you choose not to get involved and participate in this democracy, then you are abdicating your responsibility and there's no upside to that. We are all responsible for the government we have and it's time to step up to the plate.

The Reverend Dr. Martin Luther King Jr. once said "Democracy transformed from thin paper to thick action is the greatest form of government on earth." But living up to that ideal requires a certain amount of effort from all of us. It starts with trust in your elected officials which translates to trust in government. An engaged citizenry is one that trusts its government.

AUTHENTIC LISTENING

If you are considering running for elected office or if you are currently working in government, authentic listening is the single most important skill you can have in public office. It is the ability to listen to what people are saying, repeating back to them what you heard to clarify it and make sure you understood, and then responding to their concerns. It is absolutely imperative in civic engagement that we all practice authentic listening skills.

You know politicians who pretend to listen to you, nod their head, and then walk away and that's that. We need to learn as citizens not to accept that response any longer. We need to demand more of our public servants, and we need to participate more. When we planned for the Education Summit, our facilitators were trained in authentic listening skills. The ability to actually listen to someone sometimes needs to be a learned trait. Often times, people simply look like they're listening when in fact, they are really thinking about what they want to say next. That is not authentic listening. You can't just hear the words people are saying, you have to understand their meaning.

CIVIC ENGAGEMENT IN
THE 21ST CENTURY

When I first embarked on this story, it was to show that successful civic engagement based on a civil society with a desire to bring social change would come from an honest, open, and authentic process. It would be built on the words, hearts, and minds of the citizenry. But currently, civic discourse often does not come from thoughtful processes. Instead if comes from "we won, so we're right and we have all the answers." In these days of tweeting and texting, we are missing a fundamental part of engagement: the ability to digest and reflect. In our haste, we rush to the large fault lines of division, rather than the principles of unity.

The patience to hear, patience to listen, and to ask for clarity makes us fall short in a world that demands an instant response. Until we ask for clarity, the opportunity drifts and uncertainty reigns.

OUR CHALLENGE AS
A CIVIL SOCIETY

In order for civic engagement to transform communities—and make no mistake— meaningful engagement can transform communities, we must collectively see it as a priority. That means putting our money where our mouths are and having public personnel dedicated to engaging the citizenry. We cannot simply leave it up to the elected officials to decide when or whether to engage on any given issue. And we can't continue to engage only on those issues fringe talk show hosts want to focus on. We should have Centers for Civic Engagement at every public college and university in the country. City departments should have someone in the department with the skill set to work on meaningful civic engagement. When you're getting ready to launch any major initiative, the question should be, what kind of civic engagement has there been around this issue? Ideally, you should have a Department of Civic Engagement or, at the very least, a Director of Civic Engagement whose mission is to keep the citizenry informed and involved. We should be conducting research on engagement habits, what works in cities across the country, and how movements such as March For Our Lives and Black Lives Matter can move from marching to governing.

Is there a way to move people away from their computers

and get them to actually attend meetings? Well, yes—but usually it is as a last resort. Citizens show up for public policy debates mainly when they have already suffered, or feel that they are about to suffer. In other words, they'll show up if the proposed policy, or lack thereof, directly affects their lives. For example: The Seattle City Council recently passed a "head tax on business" which would have levied a tax on businesses based on the number of employees, all to alleviate homelessness. At that time the tax was hugely unpopular—so much so that just a few weeks after passing the tax, the council felt compelled to repeal it. Such actions quickly erode trust and confidence in our elected officials. The tax was touted as a solution to homelessness, but many citizens saw it as throwing more money at the problem and hurting local businesses.

When we held the Education Summit, we didn't have the advantage of social media as a platform to encourage engagement. If the city were to launch a public information campaign now around opportunities to engage on homelessness, the possibilities are endless and they could be quite successful in getting people to show up. The Seattle City Council would benefit greatly from substantial civic engagement on homelessness. It would help restore trust in their leadership while providing a platform for real, meaningful change. It is my sincere belief and observation that most people are not happy with "top down" governing when it comes to this issue. If it's the sidewalk in front of your house that holds three sleeping bags and a shopping cart full of belongings, you want to engage on this issue. If it is your son or daughter suffering from mental illness and homelessness, you want to engage on this issue. If you are a concerned citizen and a taxpayer, you want to engage on this issue. If you're an overworked and underfunded non-profit, providing services to the homeless, you want to engage on this issue. People just have to be asked, informed, and encouraged. And then, most importantly, they need to be heard.

THE OPPORTUNITIES OUR
PROBLEMS PRESENT

Every problem in society offers us the opportunity to find a solution. Let me repeat that. *Every problem in society offers us the opportunity to find a solution.* And every opportunity to find a solution rises from engagement. So, for example, if the Seattle City Council wants to tackle homelessness, it should engage the public in a way that would make our Education Summit look small in comparison. They need to find a way to promote such engagement, get the buy-in of stakeholders and critics alike, and explain to the community that it is their chance to be heard. So here are some concrete things the city could do to get the community engaged.

- Contact all those concerned with and effected by the issue and ask for their help to develop plans to bring the city together to talk about the problem. Engage the sharpest critics and ask for their help from the beginning in order to get their buy-in on how to proceed. Then provide safe places for everyone to listen authentically to the range of concerns surrounding this issue.

- Provide a meaningful feedback mechanism to ensure that participants have been heard and understood. A

118

British saying from the 1700s is often quoted to this day: "Many a man would rather you heard his story than to grant his wish." Hear these complaints. Repeat what they told you. Make sure you understand what they're saying and let them know you understand.

- Give those present an opportunity to revise and expand their comments. Hearts and minds can be changed when citizens gather to listen to one another. Allow for that organic change and honor it.

- Create a framework for implementation that includes the continuous involvement of the participants. Make citizens know that those charged with implementing change are in it for the long haul. Sustainability needs to be a big component of any proposal. This may be a critical aspect of solving homelessness since dropping the ball with services and attention is what got us here in the first place.

- Ensure that those who implement the vision represent the faces of those we serve. Diversity of experience will be critical in proposals to provide effective services, such as mental health and wellness services.

- Leaders must rally the community around the proposals and show them it is their plan. Get buy-in from the service community. Allow them to not only respond, but genuinely encourage them to listen to citizens who may not be sympathetic to the population social workers serve. Generally, it was the social service community that wanted the "head tax on local businesses" which met much opposition it later had to be repealed. Give them an opportunity to discuss their issues and where they need more funds to deal effectively with homelessness.

- Look to other communities. What innovations are being used in other communities to deal with the homeless population? Find out what works and learn how it might be applied to be successful here.

THE CHALLENGE FOR
OUR LEADERS

For those leaders who believe quick action shows leadership and a long process chills action—I would say: *Go to the people*. Listen to what they say and demonstrate you understand what they've said. Know you are building on their dreams, not yours. And when the work is done, they will say they built it themselves, which they have.

To make it work, leaders need to understand what ingredients need to be there. They need to provide the framework for creativity, authentic listening, intellectual challenges, and passion. They need to provide feedback loops and get input. Then go back and say "Here's what I'm working on. Do I have it right?"

In civic engagement, instant gratification is the enemy. Because of our insatiable need for instant gratification, too often we turn to, or go along with quick solutions. But if you truly have engagement, it means you have to have coalitions. And that takes time.

LEADERSHIP AND THE ART
OF COALITION BUILDING

Coalition building takes hard work, dedication, and time. The
very name tells you you're going to have to bring people together
from all different backgrounds, political views, economic levels,
and educational levels to work on one issue. It is how effectively
you communicate that you genuinely want their input that matters when you want to engage them. It is how you build trust.

Getting businesses, environmental advocates, mental health
experts, social justice activists, anti-tax crusaders, and both left
and right leaning political operatives all together is a feat in
itself. But if these folks don't come together in a civil, respectful,
and efficient manner, there will be no constructive engagement.
That's why learning to structure and facilitate these interac-
tions is critical. Facilitator training and selection is incredibly
important to successful engagement.

Structuring and facilitating engagement requires the where-
withal to recognize when people are protecting only the interests

of their own institutions and organizations, and recognizing when they are open to compromise and authentic listening. I would encourage any entity attempting a broad based civic engagement opportunity to take the selection of facilitators very seriously.

During the organization of the engagement event, you need to have some flexibility in recruitment of facilitators. Make sure their viewpoint is more than what their organization wants from them—that for them it's a matter of principle. It is important to remember that the more diverse the crowd, the more possible it is that the solutions and remedies that develop can be widely accepted. The broader the constituency, the more people will own the way forward.

A WAY FORWARD IN
UNCERTAIN TIMES

In 2020 our country roiled with a convergence of events not seen in this century. There was a pandemic and resulting public health crisis, a damaged economy with towering levels of unemployment, and massive protests against police violence with calls for racial justice and equality. How those in a position of leadership respond to these crises is an open question. Will they respond with solutions and public policy that can re-structure society in ways that live up to our country's promise of liberty and justice for all? Will they address disparate educational and employment opportunities and the self-perpetuating cycle of poverty? Kareem Abdul-Jabbar wrote "Racism in America is like dust in the air. It seems invisible—even if you're choking on it—until you let the sun in. Then you see it everywhere." Will this time in history be a racial reckoning, an inflection point, and offer what Ta-Nehisi Coates said to Ezra Klein in June of 2020, "I can't believe I'm gonna say this, but I see hope. I see progress right now."[51]

If the progress Coates sees is to be sustained, if it is to roll forward like the massive and diverse waves of protest that swept the nation, leaders must work tirelessly to keep citizens engaged. And a critical part of engaging citizens is inspiring them to invest in and partner in creating solutions. To do that, there is no single thing more important than gaining public trust. And to that end—they must know they are heard.

Will this time be different? I'm at heart an optimist, and so I, too, see hope.

ENDNOTES

1   "Thriving Seattle Finds Few Issues in Mayoral Race," Wallace Turner, Special to the New York Times, October 7, 1985

2   The Democrats—Jackson Supporters Are Quick to Celebrate as Caucus Produce Real Horse Race in State, Ross Anderson, Seattle Times, March 9, 1988

3   Rice Kicks Off His Campaign for Congress, Susan Gilmore, The Seattle Times, March 30, 1988

4   "Group Fights School Measure—Initiative Harms Race Relations, Prominent Black Leaders Contend, Joe Haberstroh, The Seattle Times, July 25, 1989.

5   From Norman Rice's mayoral bid announcement written by Walt Crowley, July 28, 1989

6   Sue Tupper Interview, April 2015

7   "Anti-Busing Plan Wins Favor In Poll," Joe Haberstroh, Susan Gillmore, The Seattle Times, September 25, 1989

8   Candidates....The Seattle Times

9   "In Seattle Mayoral Race, a Sense of the Possible." Tim Egan, The New York Times, November 1, 1989

10   Sue Tupper, Ed Summit conversation, April 2019

11 Bob Watt, Ed Summit conversation, April 2019

12 "The 1989 Elections: Seattle First Black Is Elected Mayor, Defeating Busing Opponent." Tim Egan, The NewYork Times, November 9, 1989

13 "Inscription is Trademark of Rice Party." Nancy Bartley, The Seattle Times, January 8, 1990

14 *Brown vs. Board of Education,* US Supreme Court Ruling, Majority Opinion by Chief Justice Earl Warren

15 School Desegregation and Equal Educational Opportunity, Civil Rights 101, Leadership Conference on Civil Rights Education Fund/2001

16 School Desegregation and Equal Educational Opportunity, Civil Rights 101, Leadership Conference on Civil Rights Education Fund/2001

17 "6 Seattle Schools Have Become Whiter As New Assignment Plan Changes Racial Balance," Seattle Times, Brian M. Rosenthal, Justin Mayo, August 21, 2012

18 "Forced Busing" Didn't Fail. Desegregation is the Best Way to Improve Our Schools." George Theoharis for the Washington Post, October 23, 2015

19 HistoryLink.org (Cassandra Tate) *"Busing in Seattle: A Well-Intentioned Failure*

20 HistoryLink.org (Cassandra Tate) *"Busing in Seattle: A Well-Intentioned Failure*

21 HistoryLink.org (Cassandra Tate) *"Busing in Seattle: A Well-Intentioned Failure"*

22 HistoryLink.org (Cassandra Tate) *"Busing in Seattle: A Well-Intentioned Failure"*

23 Sue Tupper, Ed Summit Conversation, April 2019

24 Linda Thompson-Black, Office of the Mayor, Letter to the Planning Committee, March 2, 1990

25 Ibid.

26 Linda Thompson-Black, Ed Summit Conversation, April 2019

27 Linda Thompson-Black, Office of the Mayor, Letter to the Ed Summit Planning Committee, March 2, 1990

28 Ibid.

29 Education Summit Format, draft, Office of the Mayor, March 2, 1990

30 Sue Tupper, Ed Summit conversation, April 2019

31 Laird Harris, Ed Summit conversation, April 2019

32 "Education Summit's Hopeful Start," Mindy Cameron, The Seattle Times, April 22, 1990

33 Ed Summit Conversation, April 2019

34 Bob Watt, Interview

35 "City to Place Education Tax on General-Election Ballot," Walter Hatch/Dee Norton, The Seattle Times, August 23, 1990.

36 "Rice, Billings, Unveil School Aid Plans—Property Taxes Would Be Source of Money," Paula Block, The Seattle Times, August 24, 1990.

37 "Turning the Corner—Very Encouraging signs for Seattle Schools," Editorial, The Seattle Times, October 14, 1990

38 Ibid.

39 Backers Say Proposition 1 Will Pull the "Seattle Family" Together. Cathy Reiner, The Seattle Times, October 14

40   "Many Who Ok'd Levy Don't Have Children," Paula Brock, The Seattle Times, November 14, 1990

41   "Many Who Ok'd Levy Don't Have Children," Paula Brock, The Seattle Times, November 14, 1990

42   Rice, Norman B. (b. 1943) HistoryLink.org Essay 8283, Mary T. Henry

43   "Re-Engineering Community Development for the 21st Century" Donna Fabiani and Terry F. Buss

44   "Re-Engineering Community Development for the 21st Century" Donna Fabiani and Terry F. Buss

45   "Vision, Civic Pride and Political Courage Lead to a Revitalized Downtown," Randall Bloomquist, Pine Street Group, LLC, June 7, 2016

46   "Vision, Civic Pride and Political Courage Lead to a Revitalized Downtown," Randall Bloomquist, Pine Street Group, LLC, June 7, 2016

47   "Vision, Civic Pride and Political Courage Lead to a Revitalized Downtown," Randall Bloomquist, Pine Street Group, LLC, June 7, 2016

48   Civic Collaboration: Norman Rice Talks About Effective Engagement, Anne Miano, Washington Technology Industry Association, April 15, 2017.

49   Real Change

50   Public Trust in Government: 1958-2017, Pew Research Center

51   The Ezra Klein Show, June 5, 2020

ABOUT THE AUTHOR

Norman B. Rice was Mayor of Seattle for two terms from 1990–
1998 and is regarded as one of the best mayors Seattle ever had.
He is a graduate of the Evans School of Public Policy and Governance at the University of Washington and the recipient of its
highest honor, Alumnus Summa Laude Dignatus. Together with
his wife Constance Rice, he received the American Jewish Feder-
ation's Human Relations Award and the YMCA of Greater Seattle's A.K. Guy Award which recognizes outstanding service and
dedication to social responsibility. Norm Rice is also the recipient of the Municipal League of King County's James R. Ellis
Regional Leadership Award, the Seattle Urban League's Edwin

T. Pratt Award, the King County Board of Realtors First Citizen Award, and the National Neighborhood Coalition's National Award for Leadership on Behalf of Neighborhoods. He holds honorary degrees from Seattle University, University of Puget Sound, Cornish College of the Arts, and Whitman College. A member of Barack Obama's White House Council for Community Solutions, he was the first Seattle mayor to ever become President of the U.S. Conference of Mayors.

CPSIA information can be obtained
at www.ICGtesting.com
Printed in the USA
LVHW052015120820
663009LV00022B/2473